Dallas Cowboys
Family Cookbook

DALLAS COWBOYS
VI XII XXVII · SUPER BOWL CHAMPIONS · XXVIII XXX
40th
Anniversary
1960-1999

FEATURING SPECIAL RECIPES OF CHEF GRADY SPEARS

Dallas Cowboys Wives
The Dallas Cowboys Family Cookbook

First Printing: October, 1999

Happy Hill Farm Academy/Home
HC 51, Box 56
Granbury, Texas 76048

Acknowledgments

To Gene and Jerry Jones, and to every player, coach, and Cowboys administration—plus their wives and families—who had a part in making this year's *Dallas Cowboys Family Cookbook* a reality, we give our special thanks.

Our gratitude to Brooke and Dale Hellestrae, and Laurie and Chan Gailey, who worked very hard at gathering the materials for this volume. Thanks, also, to all of the wives—players, coaches, and administration—for your cooperation in providing the materials to be used for the *Family Cookbook*.

Dallas Cowboys wives.

We're especially grateful for the encouragement and cooperation of these friends in the administrative office without whose assistance this year's *Family Cookbook* would not be: Charlotte (Jones) Anderson, Doreen Bice, Laura Fryar, Marylyn Love, Bridgette Smith, and Bill Priakos.

A special tribute to Jim Maurer, the Dallas Cowboys Head Trainer, and his wife, Rosanne. Jim is the Farm's link to the Ed Block Courage Award Foundation.

Thanks to the TV production department—John Chang, Roxanne Medina, and Scott Purcel—for their assistance in providing film for marketing.

Photography, art, and design was provided by Geno Loro and Jimmy Mowry in Fort Worth.

Our further appreciation to Russ Russell, Cheryl Harris, Ron Spain, and all of the wonderful Dallas Cowboys "Weekly" staff, for their help with production photos.

And to the two real "brains" behind the new *Family Cookbook* concept, and the folks who did most of the work: Gloria, my wife; and Stacy Gilbert, my associate.

Our thanks to Barry and Virginia Kerrigan and Del LeMond of Desktop

Miracles for designing the interior, and for handling production details.

Our special thanks to Gary Lawrence at Network Printing in Fort Worth, who printed the cookbook.

What you all have done in the creation of the all-new *Family Cookbook* is to provide Happy Hill Farm Academy/Home with a vehicle for raising money for the Farm's Scholarship Fund for indigent children. God bless each of you as we together reach out a helping hand to the hurting children around us. The *Family Cookbook* is a means to this end.

> C. EDWARD SHIPMAN
> FOUNDER
> HAPPY HILL FARM
> ACADEMY/HOME

Matt, student at Happy Hill Farm, meets David LaFleur.

Some young people from Happy Hill Farm.

IV

at Happy Hill Farm Academy/Home

Jerry and Gene Jones.

Four years ago, Jerry Jones and a group of Dallas Cowboys players came to the campus of Happy Hill Farm Academy/ Home to officially dedicate the Dallas Cowboys Courage House. The Dallas Cowboys Courage House was the sixth such home for at-risk children. Other Courage Houses are located in the following NFL cities: Detroit, Chicago, Pittsburgh, Miami, New York, Oakland, and Baltimore. The long-range goal of the Ed Block Courage Award Foundation is to establish a Courage House in every NFL city.

The partnership, embodied with the Courage House logo, represents the commitment of the NFL, NFL Charities, NFL Alumni, NFL Players Association, PFATS, and the Ed Block Courage Award Foundation. The commitment is to provide shelter, treatment, and prevention programs to victims of child abuse and domestic violence.

Each year, since 1984, the Ed Block Courage Award Foundation honors those NFL players who exemplify courage in the face of overwhelming odds. The award is usually presented to a player, voted by his peers, who has come back from some career-threaten injury to play once again.

NATIONAL SUPPORT NETWORK
©1989, Ed Block Courage Award Foundation, Inc.

v

1998 Courage Awards Dinner—
Darren Woodson and Ed Shipman.

Smith; 1997 - Tony Tolbert; and this year's (1998) winner, Darren Woodson.

Happy Hill Farm Academy/Home is pleased to be a part of this growing national organization dedicated to reaching out a helping hand to abused and neglected children.

Dallas Cowboys Recipients of the Ed Block Courage Award are as follows: 1984 - James Jones; 1985 - Howard Richards; 1986 - Anthony Dorsett; 1987 - Brian D. Baldinger; 1988 - Randy White; 1989 - Ed "Too Tall" Jones; 1990 - Kelvin Martin; 1991 - Ken Norton, Jr.; 1992 - Daryl Johnston; 1993 - Bill Bates; 1994 - Mark Stepnoski; 1995 - Erik Williams; 1996 - Kevin

Happy Hill Farm youngster.

Where Tomorrow Begins

Happy Hill Farm Academy/Home is a safe haven for children who come from backgrounds where families are unable to meet their special needs. More than 100 boys and girls, live, work, and study at Happy Hill Farm. Every child at Happy Hill Farm is in desperate need of help if they are to survive and become independent, responsible, productive, young adults. The purchase of this *Family Cookbook* is literally giving these children another chance in life.

Happy Hill Farm Academy/Home is a 500-acre working farm/campus, located southwest of Dallas/Fort Worth between Granbury and Glen Rose, Texas.

Uniqueness of the Program . . .

The Farm is different from many other child-care facilities, because Happy Hill Farm does not receive any State or Federal funds, nor United Way monies. The program is solely-funded by the private sector . . . corporations, foundations, and individuals just like you!

Happy Hill Farm Children's Home is licensed by the Texas Department of

Kids wearing face paint.

Protective and Regulatory Services. Happy Hill Farm Academy is accredited by the Southern Association of Colleges and Schools and is a member of the Texas Association of Private and Parochial Schools and the Texas Association of Non-Public Schools.

Additionally, Happy Hill Farm has a fully-accredited (K-12 grades) private school on campus. Classes are very small, and teachers are trained to work with emotionally-disturbed children. Each child receives the help necessary to succeed in school.

Who Comes to Happy Hill Farm . . .

Boys and girls, 5 to 18 years of age, are considered for admission without regard to race, religion, or ethnic origin. There are boys and girls from a variety of racial backgrounds on campus.

The Farm and the Program . . .

The 500-acre working farm/campus contains thirteen homestyle living units. Each is home to eight boys or girls. There is a husband-wife houseparent couple in each living unit. There are athletic fields, a gym, barns, dining center, vocational greenhouse, agricultural buildings, and a woodshop.

Young people of Happy Hill Farm at 1999 Dallas Cowboys Kickoff Luncheon.

The accredited private school focuses on high academic standards, but it also allows the students to participate in supplementary programs—such as art and music—each designed to impart knowledge, sharpen skills, and build self-esteem.

As a working farm, Happy Hill Farm raises its own beef, pork, and lamb. There are horses and a host of pets for the children. The 4-H program is very active. The students care for their livestock projects daily, and blue ribbons adorn the wall of the classroom. A large garden provides foodstuffs for the dining center. Additionally, the land is used to grow grain and hay crops for the livestock.

Happy Hill Farm's boys' and girls' teams excel in track, football, volleyball, basketball, and baseball while competing in the Texas Association of Private and Parochial Schools. The gym's trophy case is jammed, bearing testimony to the students' hard work and athletic abilities.

Moral and Spiritual Aspect . . .

Although the Farm is Christian and has strong moral and spiritual underpinnings, it is not connected to any church or denominational group. The highest moral, ethical, and spiritual values are taught. Children from any or no religious background are offered care.

Twenty-five Years of Blood, Sweat, and Tears . . .

It was 1974—Ed and Gloria Shipman, in their forties, lived in their country home on acreage just outside of Dallas-Fort Worth. Ed was happy in his ministry and work. Their two sons, Chuck and Todd,

Texas Governor George Bush with Farm student, Franklin.

were sixteen and fourteen years of age. The family was "comfortable." Little did they realize that a telephone call for help from a local marshall was about to change the whole course of their lives.

In response to that marshall's appeal for help, the Shipmans briefly took into their home two teenage runaway sisters. In an effort to find a permanent home for the girls, the Shipmans visited child-care facilities throughout Texas. The sisters were finally placed in a small children's home near Austin . . . but the Shipman family had been gripped emotionally. They were now aware of the desperate plight of thousands of America's hurting boys and girls—the "drop-outs" and "kicked-outs" of society.

A year later . . . 1975, with personal financial resources sufficient to last only a few years—but with, what they felt, to be a sense of Divine direction—the Shipmans opened their hearts, and officially opened the doors of Happy Hill Farm Academy/Home, to a group of young boys.

Darren Woodson visits Farm.

The Cowboy Connection . . .

In 1996, the Dallas Cowboys Courage House was dedicated on the campus of Happy Hill Farm. The Courage House is part of the Ed Block Courage Award Foundation, a national support network dedicated to helping at-risk children.

Funding . . .

Most of the children who come to the Farm have little or no money for their care. Scholarships—underwritten by individuals, clubs, corporations, and special projects—like *The Dallas Cowboys Family Cookbook*—help to pay for clothing, school books, food, and all the many things that it takes to raise healthy, happy children.

Happy Hill Farm Academy/ Home is a non-profit, charitable, Texas corporation and is operated almost entirely with contributions from the private sector. Fees and tuitions from student families account for only a small portion (less than 8%) of the Farm's annual operating budget. All gifts of money, stocks, bonds, property, or gifts-in-kind are tax-deductible.

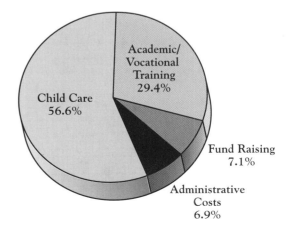

Child Care 56.6%

Academic/ Vocational Training 29.4%

Fund Raising 7.1%

Administrative Costs 6.9%

Here's How Your Gifts Are Used

Happy Hill Farm Academy/Home's Founders, Ed and Gloria Shipman, their two sons, President/CFO—Todd Shipman and COO—Chuck Shipman, and the Farm's Board of Directors believe strongly in financial accountability. The Farm utilizes the services of a recognized certified public accountant and one of the Metroplex's largest law firms. Happy Hill Farm has an annual audit. The Farm has worked tirelessly to keep these promotional costs and administrative costs to the bare minimum. Since Happy Hill Farm Academy/Home receives no State or Federal funds, nor any United Way monies, the Farm is totally dependent on the gifts from its friends in the private sector. The monies you send to Happy Hill Farm go directly to care for the children. If you wish to help financially, volunteer your time or services, or get involved in some other way, please write or call:

Happy Hill Farm
HC 51, Box 56
Granbury, Texas 76048
Phone: (254) 897-4822

Ed and Gloria Shipman with son, Chuck, Chief Operational Officer of Happy Hill Farm.

Table of Contents

Table of Contents

THE COACHES AND STAFF

NEIMAN MARCUS SALUTES

MR. AND MRS. JERRY JONES AND THE DALLAS COWBOYS FOR THEIR WORK ON BEHALF OF THE COURAGE HOUSE AT HAPPY HILL FARM.

Neiman Marcus

The Jones Family

"In the area of community service, our organization's mission is built upon an overall philosophy of helping those who don't have the strength, the resources, or the means to help themselves."
— JERRY JONES

Jerry & Gene JONES

NFL EXPERIENCE
11th year, Purchased Dallas
Cowboys, February 25, 1989

BIRTHDAY
10-13-42 — *Jerry*
2-14-42 — *Gene*

COLLEGE
Arkansas — *Jerry*
Arkansas — *Gene*

KIDS
Stephen (35), Charlotte (33),
Jerry, Jr. (30)

GRANDKIDS
Jessica Jones (6),
Jordan Jones (5),
Caroline Jones (2),
John Stephen Jones, Jr.
(newborn),
Haley Anderson (6),
Shy Anderson, Jr. (4)

Charlotte, Batman, Gene, and Shy, Jr.

If you could put your own message on a billboard for all to see, what would it be?
"Take time for your family." — *Jerry*

All children should be taught to
"Follow the Golden Rule—'Do unto others as you would have them do unto you.'" — *Jerry & Gene*

This makes me smile
"When our family is all together, and just seeing our grandchildren." — *Jerry & Gene*

My/Our plans for the future are
"To win another Super Bowl." — *Jerry & Gene*

My hero/heroes are
"My husband and children—I am so very proud of them." — *Gene*

First meal my spouse ever prepared for me
"Fried fish." — *Jerry*

Favorite food/meal
"Fried quail and mashed potatoes." — *Jerry*
"Fresh fruit salad, and biscuits and cream gravy." — *Gene*

My ideal vacation
"A boat trip with my family." — *Gene*

Jerry, Karen, Stephen Jr., Stephen, and Gene.

GREEN SALSA

10 tomatillos
1 garlic clove
½ onion

cilantro, to taste
3 jalapeños

Mix together tomatillos, jalapeños, and garlic in a saucepan; bring to a boil for about 10 minutes. While cooking, chop the onion and cilantro; set aside. After cooking, mash the tomatillos, jalapeños, and garlic together. Add onion and cilantro to salsa. Salt, to taste.

CHICKEN SOUP

1 whole, medium-size chicken
¼ pound noodles, uncooked
celery, chopped
potato, cut in quarters
carrots, cut

1 teaspoon garlic powder
1 teaspoon onion powder
1 envelope of Lipton Chicken Noodle Soup Mix
½ teaspoon celery salt

Boil chicken, until done. Once chicken is cooked, remove from the broth. Add the chopped celery, carrots, potato, and packet of Lipton Soup Mix. Add the noodles to the broth; bring to boil for about 40 minutes. Reduce heat.

While preparing the soup, remove the skin from the chicken, and debone. Add chicken to the soup 20-30 minutes before serving. Soup serves up to 8 people.

Hobbies/Other Interests
"Snow skiing." — *Jerry*

I collect
"Rare books." — *Gene*

When others describe you, what character qualities do they use?
"Very genuine and caring." — *Gene*

Haley, Jerry, and Shy, Jr.

Shy Jr., Caroline, and Gene.

3

Stephen & Karen JONES

VICE PRESIDENT / DIRECTOR OF PLAYER PERSONNEL

NFL EXPERIENCE
10th year, Dallas Cowboys

BIRTHDAY
6-21-64 — *Stephen*
8-9-64 — *Karen*

COLLEGE
Arkansas — *Stephen*
Arkansas — *Karen*

KAREN'S OCCUPATION
Housewife, mother

KIDS
Jessica (6), Jordan (5), Caroline (2), John Stephen (newborn)

Stephen with his girls—Jessica, Jordan, and Caroline.

If you could put your own message on a billboard for all to see, what would it be?
"Live every day as if it were your last!" — *Stephen & Karen*

All children should be taught to
"Love God, respect others, count your blessings, and help others who are less fortunate than you." — *Stephen & Karen*

This makes me smile
"The faces of our children." — *Stephen & Karen*

If you were stranded on a desert island, three things you would take with you
"My family, my TV, and cell phone." — *Stephen*
"My family, a great book, and my treadmill." — *Karen*

My favorite books/authors are
"John Grisham." — *Stephen & Karen*

If you could leave one thing behind for the world to learn from life, it would be
"To be good parents. It's the most important job we do." — *Stephen & Karen*

Our plans for the future are
"To enjoy our opportunity to be involved with the Cowboys, and raise our children to be independent, healthy, happy people." — *Stephen & Karen*

My hero/heroes are
"My parents." — *Stephen*
"My mother—Linda, and my sister-in-law—Barbara, because of the strength and determination they have shown in overcoming obstacles in their lives." — *Karen*

Karen with John Stephen Jones, Jr. (2 months).

4

STEPHEN'S CHICKEN FRIED STEAK

2 pounds tenderized steak
1/2 cup vegetable oil
3 tablespoons sugar
1/2 teaspoon salt
1 egg
1 tablespoon baking powder

1 1/2 cups milk
1/4 stick butter, or margarine
2 cups milk
1/8 cup vegetable cooking oil
1/4 cup flour
1/2 teaspoon salt

Cut steak into 6 to 8 pieces. Flour each piece thoroughly; shake off excess. Dip in batter, and flour again; shake off excess flour. Preheat oil; cook meat 7 to 10 minutes, until golden brown.

BATTER: Mix sugar, salt, egg, baking powder, and half of the milk; stir, until smooth. Add remainder of milk, and mix well.

GRAVY: Melt butter; add 2 cups milk, and mix thoroughly. Bring to a boil. Blend flour into oil; add to heated milk. Stir, until smooth and thickened. Remove from heat; add salt and pepper, to taste.

KAREN'S FAVORITE CHEESE RING

1 pound sharp Cheddar cheese, grated
1 cup pecans, chopped
2 cups mayonnaise
1 onion, finely-chopped

1 garlic clove, pressed
1/2 teaspoon Tabasco
1 cup strawberry jam or preserves

Mix cheese, pecans, mayonnaise, onion, garlic, and Tabasco thoroughly. Place in a margarine-greased ring mold. Refrigerate overnight. Unmold onto serving plate; place strawberry jam in the center. Serve with crackers.

First meal my spouse ever prepared for me

"Country dinner—chicken fried steak with gravy, mashed potatoes, and green beans." — *Stephen*

"Steak." — *Karen*

Favorite food/meal

"Steak and pasta." — *Stephen*

"Chinese food from P. F. Chang." — *Karen*

I wish I could sing like

"Elton John." — *Stephen*

"Barbra Streisand." — *Karen*

John Stephen Jones, Jr. (2 1/2 months).

My friends call me (nickname)

"Jonesy." — *Stephen*

My ideal vacation

"On the beach or in the mountains with my wife and children." — *Stephen*

"On the beach in Florida with Stephen and our children." — *Karen*

Hobbies/Other Interests

"Coaching my girls' soccer teams, running, and snow skiing." —*Stephen*

"Running, reading, and volunteering at my children's school." — *Karen*

I collect

"Sports memorabilia." — *Stephen*

"Antiques, Limoge boxes, and teapots." — *Karen*

My wife, mother, grandmothers, are special because

"They are all incredible mothers. " — *Stephen*

5

ANDERSON

VICE PRESIDENT / DIRECTOR OF MARKETING AND SPECIAL EVENTS

BIRTHDAY
7-26-66 — *Charlotte*
4-3-63 — *Shy*

COLLEGE
Stanford — *Charlotte*
Arkansas — *Shy*

SHY'S OCCUPATION
President, Alitel
Communications

KIDS
Haley (6), Shy, Jr. (4)

PETS
Star and Champ -
Chocolate Labs

Charlotte and Shy.

All children should be taught to
"Respect their elders, each other, and themselves." — *Charlotte*
"Be responsible for their actions." — *Shy*

This makes me smile
"My children." — *Charlotte & Shy*

My hero/heroes are
"My parents." — *Charlotte*

If you were stranded on a desert island, three things you would take with you
"My husband and my two children." — *Charlotte*
"My family, and some Bullfrog sunscreen for Shybo." — *Shy*

If you could leave one thing behind for the world to learn from life, it would be
"Life is too short to worry about the small things. Make the most of every day." — *Charlotte*
"Focus on the things that you can make a difference in—not what is out of your control." — *Shy*

My favorite books/authors are
"I enjoy a wide variety of authors." — *Charlotte*
"Stuart Woods." — *Shy*

First meal my spouse ever prepared for me
"Cheeseburgers!" — *Charlotte*
"Meatloaf." — *Shy*

Haley and Shy, Jr.

AUNT KATHY'S BLACKBERRY COBBLER

1½ tablespoons cornstarch	½ cup water
¼ cup brown sugar, packed	1½ tablespoons margarine
¼ cup white sugar (more, if berries are sour)	2 cups blackberries

Add cornstarch, brown sugar, white sugar, and water to a saucepan; heat, until thick. Add margarine and blackberries.

Pour into a baking dish. Cover with 2 layers of ready-made pie crusts. Dot top of crusts with margarine, and sprinkle sugar over the top. Bake at 450 degrees, until crust is brown.

NANA'S HOMEMADE STUFFING

1 pound Jimmy Dean Sausage	½ stick butter, melted
1 8-ounce package Pepperidge Farm Stuffing	1 onion, finely-chopped
1 heaping tablespoon sage	1 egg
1 heaping tablespoon poultry seasoning	

Cook sausage in skillet. Add onion; cook, until opaque.

Put stuffing in a large bowl; pour in sausage and onion mixture—include fat. Add seasonings, egg, and butter. Mix together with hands. If too dry, add small amount of water. If too wet, add more stuffing.

Stuff into turkey or hen, and cook, until bird is done. The stuffing can be cooked alone in pan at 350 degrees for about 30 minutes.

Favorite food/meal

"Italian—
I love pasta!" — *Charlotte*

"Thai, pizza, and
Tex-Mex." — *Shy*

I wish I could sing like

"Barbra Streisand." — *Charlotte*

"Lou Rawls." — *Shy*

My friends call me (nickname)

"Char." — *Charlotte*

"Shybo." — *Shy*

My ideal vacation

"Somewhere on a beach
with my family . . . and no
telephones!" — *Charlotte*

"Simple, easy, warm, and
sunny." — *Shy*

Hobbies/Other Interests

"Skiing, cooking, reading, and
exercising." — *Charlotte*

"Exercising, golf, hunting,
and dogs (2 labs)." —*Shy*

Haley, Charlotte, and Shy, Jr. at Texas Stadium.

I collect

"Lladro, silver goblets, and
old books." — *Charlotte*

**When others describe you,
what character qualities do
they use?**

"Self-starter, determined,
and creative." — *Charlotte*

"Competitive, assertive,
and even-tempered." —
Shy

**My husband, is special
because**

"He is extremely patient
and supportive, and he is a
great father. " — *Charlotte*

My wife, is special because

"She puts all of her energy
and love into her family—
she has her mother's
traits." — *Shy*

**I am thankful my parents/
grandparents taught me**

"To be thankful for every
day!" — *Charlotte*

"Strong values." — *Shy*

Jerry
JONES, JR.

VICE PRESIDENT / LEGAL OPERATIONS

BIRTHDAY
9-27-69

COLLEGE
Georgetown (B.A.) & SMU
(Juris Doctorate)

PETS
Saltwater aquarium with
tropical fish

Tanya Clark and Jerry, Jr.

If you could put your own message on a billboard for all to see, what would it be?
"God is first, others are second, I am third."

All children should be taught to
"Believe in themselves."

This makes me smile
"Spending time with my family."

If you were stranded on a desert island, three things you would take with you
"Plenty of food, water, and a mobile phone."

If you could leave one thing behind for the world to learn from life, it would be
"My Bible."

My/Our plans for the future are
"To get married, and raise a family of my own."

My hero/heroes are
"My grandfathers, and my father."

My favorite books/authors are
"John Grisham, Jeffrey Archer, Nelson Demille, and *To Kill a Mockingbird*."

Jerry Wayne Monty, Jerry, Jr., Stephen, and Jerry.

8

SUMMER BRUSCHETTA DIP

$3/4$ - 1 cup extra virgin cold-pressed olive oil
$1/2$ cup balsamic vinegar
$1/2$ cup fresh basil leaves, chopped
3 tablespoons garlic, finely-chopped
1 medium-size tomato, chopped
1 teaspoon salt

$1/2$ teaspoon freshly-ground pepper
2 tablespoons fresh oregano leaves, finely-chopped (optional)
1 fresh loaf of Ciabatta bread, olive oil boule, or French baguette sliced into dip-size pieces

Combine all ingredients in a serving bowl; stir, until nicely mixed. Serve with a fresh loaf or two of the suggested breads, or any fresh bread of your choice. It is ready to serve, or can be chilled for $1/2$ - 1 hour before serving. Serves 4 to 6 people.

This is a delicious dip, quick, easy to prepare, and a wonderful summer appetizer for family and friends to enjoy.

Favorite food/meal
"Fried pork chops, mashed potatoes, and blackeyed peas."

I wish I could sing like
"Frank Sinatra."

My friends call me (nickname)
"Jerome."

My ideal vacation
"A vacation at our Destin, Florida, home with our entire family."

Hobbies/Other Interests
"Tropical fish and aquariums, scuba diving, hunting, and exercise."

When others describe you, what character qualities do they use?
"Fun, charismatic, perfectionist, and spontaneous."

I collect
"Wine labels, and silver chalices."

My mother, is special because
"She has a true heart of gold."

I am thankful my parents/grandparents taught me
"The finest steel goes through the hottest furnace."

Tanya Clark, Pat Chambers, Jerry, Jr., Betty Sloan, and Gene.

Chan Gailey

With each challenge and opportunity, Chan Gailey has displayed the character, consistency, and performance of a winner.

Chan & Laurie GAILEY

NFL EXPERIENCE
12th year, Denver Broncos (6),
Pittsburgh Steelers (4),
Dallas Cowboys (2)

BIRTHDAY
1-5-52 — *Chan*
2-7-53 — *Laurie*

COLLEGE
Florida — *Chan*
Georgia Southwestern;
Florida — *Laurie*

LAURIE'S OCCUPATION
Housewife

KIDS
Tate (23), Andrew (19)

PETS
Maggie - Yellow Lab

Chan and Laurie Gailey.

All children should be taught to
"Respect others." — *Chan*
"Treat others the way they would like to be treated." — *Laurie*

This makes me smile
"My wife." — *Chan*
"Watching a child play and explore." — *Laurie*

If you were stranded on a desert island, three things you would take with you
"Bible, food, and tools." — *Chan*
"Bible, ESPN, and Diet Coke." — *Laurie*

Our plans for the future are
"Retire to north Georgia, and travel." — *Chan & Laurie*

My hero/heroes are
"My dad." — *Chan*
"My husband and my parents." — *Laurie*

My favorite books/authors are
"Frank Peretti; John Grisham." — *Chan*
"Philip Yancey." — *Laurie*

First meal my spouse ever prepared for me
"Chili." — *Chan*
"Brunswick Stew." — *Laurie*

The whole family—Chan, Maggie, Laurie, Tate, Andrew, and the puppies.

12

AUNT LIB'S FRESH COCONUT CAKE

1 fresh coconut, grated
1 8-ounce carton sour cream
1¼ cups sugar
1 box Duncan Hines Yellow Cake Mix
1 4-ounce box instant vanilla pudding

½ cup cooking oil
1 cup water
1 teaspoon vanilla flavoring
2 eggs
2 egg yolks

Icing
2 egg whites
2¾ cups sugar
3⅓ cups white karo
1 tablespoon water

5¼ teaspoons cream of tartar
6¼ teaspoons vanilla
grated coconut

To crack the coconut, punch holes in "eyes," and drain the juice. Use a hammer to crack the shell, and break coconut open. Then, pry meat away from shell with knife or screw driver. Remove brown skin from meat with vegetable peeler or knife. Shred with grater or food processor.

Combine about 1 cup of grated coconut, 8 ounces sour cream, and 1¼ cups sugar. Set aside for filling.

In a mixing bowl, combine cake mix, vanilla pudding, cooking oil, water, eggs, and vanilla. Beat, until smooth. Pour into 2 greased and floured 9-inch cake pans, Bake at 350 degrees for 30 minutes.

Allow to cool for 10 minutes on racks. Split layers to make 4. Spread filling between layers while warm. Ice cake with seven-minute icing. Press remaining coconut on sides and top of cake.

For icing, combine first 6 ingredients in double boiler, beating on high speed for 6 or 7 minutes, until soft peaks form. Remove from heat; beat, until spreading consistency.

Favorite food/meal

"Brunswick Stew, and ice cream." — *Chan*

"Sushi." — *Laurie*

I wish I could sing like

"Larnelle Harris." — *Chan*

"Babbie Mason." — *Laurie*

My ideal vacation

"5 days of golf—36 holes a day
at great courses." — *Chan*

"Driving the backroads of New England,
antiquing, and bed and breakfasts." — *Laurie*

Hobbies/Other Interests

"Golf, racquetball, and reading." — *Chan*

"Tennis, and reading." — *Laurie*

I collect

"Copper lustreware, and 'yard-long' pictures." — *Laurie*

When others describe you, what character qualities do they use?

"Compassionate." — *Laurie*

My mother, is special because

"She loved me and always believed in me." — *Chan*

My husband, is special because

"He puts others first." — *Laurie*

If I were not playing football, I'd be a

"Teacher." — *Chan*

Chan and his boys, Tate and Andrew
at training camp.

13

Grady Spears

A number of the recipes that appear in this cookbook are courtesy of Chef Grady Spears, from his book, *A Cowboy in the Kitchen*, from Ten Speed Press.

"I learned what I know about food hanging around campfires with cowboy cooks."
— GRADY SPEARS

Grady & Sara
SPEARS

BIRTHDAY
8-28-68 — *Grady*

SARA'S OCCUPATION
Keeping Grady in line!

PETS
Lucy - Weimaraner
Hershey - cat

Grady and Sara Spears.

If you could put your own message on a billboard for all to see, what would it be?
"I love Texas." — *Grady*
"Enjoy each day." — *Sara*

All children should be taught to
"Be good to other people." — *Grady*
"Respect others." — *Sara*

This makes me smile
"Good food." — *Grady*
"Babies, great meal, wonderful friendships, and a fantastic family." — *Sara*

If you were stranded on a desert island, three things you would take with you
"Lone Star beer, side of beef, and Texas music (Pat Green, Robert Earl Keene, etc.)." — *Grady*
"Husband, telephone, and lots of food—especially junk food." — *Sara*

If you could leave one thing behind for the world to learn from life, it would be
"To be good to other people." — *Grady*
"Appreciate every day." — *Sara*

Our plans for the future are
"More cookbooks, fishing, and PBS cooking series." — *Grady & Sara*

My hero/heroes are
"My family—wife, parents, sisters, brother-in-laws, etc." — *Grady*

My favorite books/authors are
"Cookbooks." — *Grady*
"Authors: Amy Tan and Ernest Hemingway. Books: *The Geisha Girl, Ya-Ya Sisterhood, You Never Know,* and *The Honk & Holler.*" — *Sara*

First meal my spouse ever prepared for me
"Sandwiches." — *Grady*

Favorite food/meal
"Fried chicken and tacos on the street in Mexico." — *Grady*
"Chips and salsa; anything Italian." — *Sara*

I wish I could sing like
"Johnny Cash." — *Grady*
"Whitney Houston, Mariah Carey, and Edie Brickell." — *Sara*

16

Chef Grady Spears's

BOCK-BATTERED QUAIL WITH CIDER ADOBO

BOCK BEER BATTER
1 cup club soda
1 cup Shiner Bock, or any good bock beer
1 teaspoon kosher salt
pinch of crushed red pepper flakes
1¾ cups flour

4 semi-boned quail, cut into quarters
6 cups peanut oil
1 cup Cider Adobo (page 40)

To prepare the beer batter, combine the soda, beer, salt, and red pepper flakes in a large, stainless steel bowl. Using a whisk, gradually add the flour, blending to avoid lumps. Stick your finger into the batter. If the batter is thick and sticks to your finger, it is ready. Add more flour if the batter seems thin.

To prepare the quail, heat 2½ to 3 inches of oil in a large, heavy skillet to 350 degrees (when a drop of batter sizzles when dropped in the oil). A deep-fat fryer may also be used, but it will take more oil to fill. Dip each piece of quail into the batter, and slide it into the oil. Do as many pieces as possible, without crowding or letting the temperature drop. Cook the quail about 8 to 10 minutes, turning once. Remove the quail to a paper towel-lined sheet pan to drain. Serve 4 pieces of quail, drizzled with the Cider Adobo, to each person. Yield: 4 servings.

My friends call me (nickname)

"Grit; Pooh." — *Grady*

"Sara—pretty original!" — *Sara*

My ideal vacation

"Fishing on the Texas Coast or Mexico." — *Grady*

"Villa in Italy or Spain, soaking up rays, and relaxing." — *Sara*

Hobbies/Other Interests

"Fishing." — *Grady*

"Running, reading, and shopping." — *Sara*

I collect

"Junk, cookbooks, and fishing gear." — *Grady*

"Mexican trinkets, and religious art." — *Sara*

Grady and Sara.

When others describe you, what character qualities do they use?

"Redneck." — *Grady*

"Upbeat and 'happy-go-lucky.'" — *Sara*

My mother, is special because

"She has supported me through everything (bad or good)." — *Grady*

My mother, is special because

"She is the smartest, most creative, and sensible person I know. She is the mold that keeps our family together." — *Sara*

If I were not a chef, I'd be a

"I'd be a cowboy." — *Grady*

I am thankful my parents/ grandparents taught me

"Work ethic." — *Grady*

"Values and morals." — *Sara*

17

Bank One is proud to support the Dallas Cowboys Courage House and Happy Hill Farm Academy/Home

To One.

Official Bank of the Dallas Cowboys

Players

Maximizing the 'magic' of the Dallas Cowboys celebrity, and using that influence to assist others through community service, is the backbone of the organization's mission away from the field of competition.

76

Flozell ADAMS

NFL EXPERIENCE
2nd year, Dallas Cowboys

BIRTHDAY
5-18-75

COLLEGE
Michigan State

My friends call me (nickname)
"The Hotel."

Adams was a key part of the line that allowed just 19 quarterback sacks in 1998—the fewest in the NFL.

Chef Grady Spears's
CHIPOTLE MEATLOAF

2 pounds ground chuck
1 cup diced red bell pepper
1 cup finely-chopped onion
2 scallions, thinly-sliced
2 tablespoons roasted garlic
    or 5 cloves garlic, minced
1 chipotle pepper
1 tablespoon adobo sauce reserved from the
    chipotle can

1 tablespoon Worcestershire sauce
3 eggs
$1/2$ cup bread crumbs
1 teaspoon Reata Grill Blend (page 64)
kosher salt, to taste
freshly-ground pepper, to taste

Preheat the oven to 350 degrees. Mix all of the ingredients in a large bowl.

Shape the mixture; put it in a loaf pan (approximately $8^{1}/_2$ by $4^{1}/_2$ by $2^{1}/_2$ inches). Cover the loaf with foil; bake for 1 to $1^{1}/_4$ hours.

Remove the foil toward the end of the baking time, if you want the top of the loaf to brown. When the meatloaf is finished baking, remove it from the oven, and let it stand for 15 minutes before serving. Unmold the loaf; slice it into serving pieces. Serve warm.

National Door Industries, Inc.

Fort Worth, Texas

"the end of the homely looking garage door"

To locate a dealer near you, visit our website at
www.natdoor.com

We are honored to be a part of the successful program that Ed and Gloria
and all of the Farm's friends have created at Happy Hill Farm Academy/Home.
Your support will help change the lives of troubled youth by providing them
with spiritual guidance, a stable atmosphere for learning, and assist them
to become successful and productive citizens in the community.

NFL EXPERIENCE
11th year, Dallas Cowboys

BIRTHDAY
11-21-66 — *Troy*
11-1-68 — *Rhonda*

COLLEGE
UCLA — *Troy*

KIDS
Rachel (9)

Troy Aikman and Rhonda Worthey.

All children should be taught to
"Be respectful of others." — *Troy*
"Be responsible for their actions, and to 'do unto others as you would have them do unto you.'" — *Rhonda*

This makes me smile
"Knowing you've helped another." — *Troy*
"Spending time with loved ones." — *Rhonda*

If you were stranded on a desert island, three things you would take with you
"Golf clubs, golf balls, and a practice net." — *Troy*
"A hammock, books, and my toothbrush." — *Rhonda*

If you could leave one thing behind for the world to learn from life, it would be
"To realize how short and precious life really is." — *Troy*
"To live each day to the fullest, and never take anything for granted." — *Rhonda*

Our plans for the future are
"To win a fourth Super Bowl, and raise a family." — *Troy & Rhonda*

My hero/heroes are
"Those people that make a difference in the world." — *Troy*

My favorite books/authors are
"Non-fiction and biographies." — *Troy*
"John Grisham to Jane Austen, and everything in between." — *Rhonda*

Favorite food/meal
"Mexican (fajitas); Mom's meatloaf; and sushi." — *Troy*
"Fajitas, pasta, and my grandma's chocolate cake." — *Rhonda*

I wish I could sing like
"Joe Avezzano or Alan Jackson." — *Troy*
"Faith Hill." — *Rhonda*

My friends call me (nickname)
"Roy." — *Troy*

HONEY-GARLIC CHICKEN PIECES

6 assorted chicken pieces, such as breasts and legs
¾ cup brown sugar
2 teaspoons dry mustard powder

4 cloves garlic, minced
3 tablespoons soy sauce
1½ cups honey

Preheat oven to 350 degrees. Rinse chicken pieces under cool water; pat dry. Place chicken in a roasting pan or Pyrex dish. Choose a pan that's just big enough so that the chicken fits in snugly. Evenly distribute the ingredients in the order they appear on the list of ingredients, finishing with the honey.

Place the dish on the middle rack of the preheated oven, uncovered, and bake for 40 to 50 minutes. Flip pieces over halfway through baking. Using a large spoon or a baster, baste the chicken every 10 minutes with the juices in the pan. Turn pieces over so that they are right side up for the final 10 minutes of baking.

Serve with a side of noodles or rice and a vegetable stir-fry. Finger-lickin' good!

LEMON CAKE

1 cup water
1 box lemon Jello
4 eggs
¾ cup Wesson oil
2 teaspoons vanilla

1 box Duncan Hines Yellow Cake Mix
2½ lemons, to squeeze for juice
1 stick margarine
2 cups powdered sugar

Heat water; dissolve lemon Jello in it. Cool.

Put eggs in mixer; beat real good at high speed. Add Wesson oil and vanilla. Add cake mix. Mix well; pour into a well-greased and floured sheet pan. Bake at 350 degrees for 40 minutes.

While cake is baking, make the filling. Cream margarine and sugar well; add lemon juice. Spread on the cake as soon as you take it from the oven.

My ideal vacation

"Anywhere with a beach, ocean, and golf." — *Troy*

"Anywhere with an ocean, white sandy beaches, and beautiful sunsets." — *Rhonda*

Hobbies/Other Interests

"Golf, computer, reading, and photography." — *Troy*

"Being a mom, working out, reading, and cooking." — *Rhonda*

Troy and Rhonda with Troy's sisters and brothers-in-law—Mike Powell, Terri Starns, David Starns, and Tammy Powell in Maui, 1999.

I collect
"Hummels." — *Troy*

When others describe you, what character qualities do they use?
"Intense and loyal." — *Troy*
"Kind-hearted, sincere, and easy-going." — *Rhonda*

My mother, is special because
"She sacrificed to be a mom and raise three children. " — *Troy*

My fiancé, is special because
"He is the most caring and thoughtful man I know. He always goes out of his way to help others." — *Rhonda*

I am thankful my parents/ grandparents taught me
"Discipline and proper manners— and to be respectful of others." — *Troy*
"That it is better to give than to receive, and The Golden Rule." — *Rhonda*

23

73

Larry & Janelle ALLEN

ALL-PRO GUARD • 6' 3" • 326

NFL EXPERIENCE
6th year, Dallas Cowboys

BIRTHDAY
11-27-71 — *Larry*
5-7-71 — *Janelle*

COLLEGE
Sonoma State — *Larry*

KIDS
Jayla Lee (4), Larry, III (3)

In just five NFL seasons, Larry Allen is already a four-time All-Pro selection—three times at guard, and once at tackle.

If I were not playing football, I'd be a
"Boxer." — *Larry*

Favorite food/meal
"Steak and French fries." — *Larry*

My ideal vacation
"Las Vegas." — *Larry*

Hobbies/Other Interests
"Fishing and traveling." — *Larry*

Larry has never missed a game, playing in 88 consecutive—including playoffs.

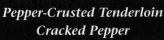
Chef Grady Spears's

PEPPER-CRUSTED TENDERLOIN WITH PORT

¹/₃ cup Cracked Pepper (recipe follows)
kosher salt, to taste
4 beef tenderloin steaks (10 to 12 ounces each)
3 tablespoons vegetable oil
2 cups port

2 tablespoons roasted shallots or 1 large shallot,
   minced
3 tablespoons honey
3 tablespoons butter

Preheat the oven to 500 degrees. Press the salt and pepper evenly into the surfaces of the steaks. Heat the oil in a large, heavy sauté pan, over high heat. Place the steaks in the pan without crowding (this may have to be done in batches); cook them, uncovered, for 3 minutes on each side. Remove the steaks to a sheet pan; place them in the oven to finish cooking (about 8 minutes for medium rare). While the steaks are in the oven, pour the port into the pan the steaks were cooked in, and reduce by half. Add the shallots and honey; stir until they are well-blended.

Remove the steaks from the oven; allow them to rest for 5 minutes. Whisk the butter into the port mixture; add salt, to taste.

Place each steak on a plate, pour the port sauce evenly over the steaks, and serve.

Yield: 4 servings.

CRACKED PEPPER

Cracked pepper is very different from freshly-ground pepper. The aroma and flavor of the peppercorn comes through in every bite.

To make cracked pepper, you need to crush each peppercorn into no more than eight or ten pieces. You can put whole peppercorns in a large frying pan and use a smaller frying pan to crush them, but you really need to bear down hard . . . this takes a lot of strength.

The easiest cracking method is to put the peppercorns in a food processor and pulse it once or twice. This method takes patience and usually requires several batches. You have to sort through the cracked peppercorns, remove the remaining whole peppercorns, and repeat the process.

The simplest way to keep cracked peppercorns in your chuck box is to buy a bottle of whole black peppercorns, crack them all, and return them to the same bottle for storage.

86 *Eric* BJORNSON

TIGHT END • 6' 4" • 236

NFL EXPERIENCE
5th year, Dallas Cowboys

BIRTHDAY
12-15-71

COLLEGE
Washington

Daryl Johnston and Eric at Wimbledon.

All children should be taught to
"Never give up."

This makes me smile
"Dogs."

My hero/heroes are
"My parents."

Favorite food/meal
"Pasta."

My friends call me (nickname)
"Bjorny (Hud calls me 'Borny')."

Hobbies/Other Interests
"Golf, movies, and water-skiing."

My mother, is special because
"She is genuine, caring, and extremely fun. "

If I were not playing football, I'd be a
"A guy looking for a job."

Eric with family in Lake Tahoe.

Chef Grady Spears's
VENISON CHILI

¹/₄ cup oil
1¹/₂ pounds venison chili meat
1 cup Red Chile Paste (see page 50)
1 red onion, chopped
2 tablespoons roasted garlic, or minced garlic
1 tablespoon Pasilla Powder (see page 142), or
    chili powder

2 teaspoons kosher salt
1 tablespoon Tabasco™ Jalapeño Sauce
1 teaspoon Mexican oregano
1 teaspoon ground cumin
3 cups chicken stock

Heat the oil in a stew pot. Add the chili meat; cook, until it is browned. Add the chile paste, onion, roasted or minced garlic, pasilla powder, salt, Tabasco™ Jalapeño Sauce, oregano, and cumin. Cook for 5 minutes, or until the onion is wilted. Add the chicken stock; simmer for 45 minutes to 1 hour, or until the venison is tender. Serve hot.

Yield: 6 servings.

I am thankful my parents/ grandparents taught me

"To work hard."

David LaFleur, Toby Gowin, and Eric aboard the U.S.S. Constellation.

Chris BRAZZELL

WIDE RECEIVER • 6' 2" • 198

NFL EXPERIENCE
1st year, Dallas Cowboys

BIRTHDAY
5-22-76

COLLEGE
Angelo State

Chris Brazzell is an avid video game player.

Chef Grady Spears's
GRILLED STRIP STEAK WITH CILANTRO BUTTER

¹/₄ cup Worcestershire sauce
¹/₄ cup olive oil
4 strip steaks (about 14 ounces each)

4 teaspoons Reata Grill Blend (page 64)
4 slices Cilantro Butter (page 191)

Prepare and heat a grill. Mix the Worcestershire sauce and olive oil in a shallow pan. Soak the steaks in this mixture, while the grill is heating. Remove from marinade; season with Reata Grill Blend. When the grill feels hot to a hand held 5 inches over the fire, it is ready to use.

Place the steaks on the grill; cook them for 5 minutes on each side, for medium. Top each steak with a cold slice of Cilantro Butter. Serve immediately.

Yield: 4 servings.

House key.
Car key.

Pump key.

You have a key to your house. You have a key to your car. Now Mobil gives you the key to the pump. With *Speedpass*, getting gas just got a little more exciting. All you have to do is wave it at the pump, gas up and go. Fast and easy. Link it to a major credit card or check card that you *already* have. And you can even specify whether you want a receipt or not. Just call toll-free **1-877-MY MOBIL** or visit mobil.com/speedpass to enroll. So join over 2 million people who already use *Speedpass*. It's safe, secure and best of all...it's free.

Mobil®

The fastest way to get gas.

60 *Chris* BRYMER

OFFENSIVE LINEMAN • 6' 3" • 300

NFL EXPERIENCE
1st year, Dallas Cowboys

BIRTHDAY
11-29-74

COLLEGE
Southern California

Brymer spent the spring of 1999 playing
with the Rhein Fire of NFL Europe.

Chef Grady Spears's
ROASTED GAME HENS WITH MOLASSES RUB

2 quarts water
6 tablespoons kosher salt
4 tablespoons whole black peppercorns
8 sprigs thyme
12 cloves garlic, minced

2 tablespoons sugar
4 whole game hens
2 tablespoons unsalted butter, softened
1 cup Molasses Rub (page 163)

Prepare a brine by mixing the water with the salt, pepper, thyme, garlic, and sugar in a container large enough to hold the game hens. A 2-gallon zipper-top plastic bag works well. Rinse the game hens. Then, submerge them in the brine. Set them aside in the refrigerator for at least 2 hours, or overnight.

To roast the hens, preheat the oven to 350 degrees. Remove the hens from the brine; pat them dry. Rub them all over with the softened butter, and place them in a roasting pan. Bake the hens for 45 minutes, basting them occasionally with pan juices. Test for doneness with a meat thermometer inserted into the thigh. It should register 160 degrees. The hens should be golden brown. Remove the hens from the oven; set them aside to rest.

Preheat the broiler. Pat Molasses Rub on the hens, packing well, to form a coating. Place the hens under the broiler, until the rub caramelizes and darkens (about 5 minutes). Remove, and serve.

Walls Industries

Salutes

The Dallas Cowboys Courage House
at
Happy Hill Farm Academy/Home

For Helping Today's Youth Find A Happier Tomorrow

1905 North Main • Cleburne, TX 76031 • (817) 645-0362

Hayward CLAY

TIGHT END • 6' 3" • 260

NFL EXPERIENCE
3rd year, Dallas Cowboys

BIRTHDAY
7-25-73

COLLEGE
Texas A&M

KIDS
Hayward, III (4)

If you could put your own message on a billboard for all to see, what would it be?
"Work hard; never ever quit."

All children should be taught to
"Humility and respect."

This makes me smile
"My family."

My plans for the future are
"To get married, and have children."

My hero/heroes are
"My dad."

My favorite books/authors are
"Science fiction."

Favorite food/meal
"Momma's meatloaf."

My friends call me (nickname)
"Big Wood."

My ideal vacation
"A cruise to the islands."

Hobbies/Other Interests
"Basketball."

When others describe you, what character qualities do they use?
"Cool."

Clay received his degree in agricultural economics in the spring of 1999.

Chef Grady Spears's
POT ROAST WITH YAMS

½ cup flour
1 teaspoon kosher salt
1 teaspoon Cracked Pepper (page 25)
4 to 6 pounds chuck roast
½ cup corn oil
¾ cup Ancho Ketchup (page 146)

3 carrots, peeled and cut in 2-inch rounds
3 East Texas yams or sweet potatoes,
    cut into 2-inch pieces
1 onion, coarsely-chopped
4 garlic cloves
2 cups beef stock

Season the flour with salt and pepper; blend thoroughly. Roll the pot roast in the flour-and-salt mixture. Heat the oil in an ovenproof stew pot large enough to cover the pot roast. Sear the roast for 4 minutes on each side, or until well-browned. Add the ketchup, carrots, sweet potatoes, onion, and garlic. Cook the stew for 5 minutes. Add the beef stock, and cover. Place the pan in a 300-degree oven; cook for 2½ to 3 hours, or until the beef is very tender.

Yield: 6 to 8 servings.

My mother and grandmother, are special because
"They raised 7 and 9 kids. "

If I were not playing football, I'd be a
"Coach."

I am thankful my parents/grandparents taught me
"To think and act respectfully."

52 *Dexter* COAKLEY

LINEBACKER • 5' 10" • 228

NFL EXPERIENCE
3rd year, Dallas Cowboys

BIRTHDAY
10-20-72

COLLEGE
Appalachian State

Dexter has provided a spark for the Cowboys defensive unit two years running.

If you could put your own message on a billboard for all to see, what would it be?
"Yes, I can."

All children should be taught to
"Obey and respect."

This makes me smile
"Seeing my family and friends happy."

If you could leave one thing behind for the world to learn from life, it would be
"The Bible."

My/Our plans for the future are
"Marry my girlfriend, and have a family."

My hero is
"My father."

My favorite books/authors are
"The Bible."

Favorite food/meal
"20-ounce porterhouse steak—cooked medium, with a loaded baked potato."

I wish I could sing like
"Ron Isley."

My friends call me (nickname)
"D.C."

My ideal vacation
"Two weeks in the Virgin Islands, with the lady of my life."

Hobbies/Other Interests
"Fishing and golfing."

I collect
"Sports cards."

AIKMAN FAN CLUB

$35

PROCEEDS BENEFIT
THE TROY AIKMAN
FOUNDATION

www.aikman.com

- ✷ 8x10 PHOTOGRAPH
- ✷ FOOTBALL CARDS
- ✷ TROY'S TEAM CAP
- ✷ TROY'S TEAM T-SHIRT
- ✷ PENNANT
- ✷ CONTESTS
- ✷ MEMBERSHIP CARD
- ✷ OTHER COWBOY GOODIES

To order call **1-800-876-9468**
or fill out membership form below.

Troy's Team Membership Form

Name _____

Address _____

City _____ State _____ Zip _____

Telephone: ( ) _____ Birthdate: ___/___/___

E-mail: _____ T-Shirt Size Youth: S, M, L, XL.

Payment options (check one)   Adult: M, L, XL, XXL.

❏ Visa   ❏ MasterCard   ❏ American Express
     ❏ Discover   ❏ Check   ❏ Money Order

Card No. _____ Exp. Date: __/

DL No. (If paying by check) _____

Signature: _____

Your annual membership fee of $35.00 includes the following items: Troy's Team 8x10 Photograph, T-shirt, Hat, Pennant, Membership Card, UpperDeck Football Cards and other goodies. **To join Troy's Team, mail membership form and payment information to: Calvert Direct, P.O. Box 851, Colleyville, Tx 76034 call 1-800-876-9468.**

Richie & Kristin CUNNINGHAM

KICKER • 5' 10" • 167

NFL EXPERIENCE
3rd year, Dallas Cowboys

BIRTHDAY
8-18-70 — *Richie*
3-17-71 — *Kristin*

COLLEGE
Southwestern
Louisiana — *Richie*
Northern Arizona
University — *Kristin*

KRISTIN'S OCCUPATION
Speech Pathologist

PETS
Sasha and Sadie — cats;
Opie and Kady — dogs

Kristin and Richie honeymooning in Maui.

If you could put your own message on a billboard for all to see, what would it be?
"Be kind to one another." — *Richie*
"Treat others as you want to be treated." — *Kristin*

All children should be taught to
"All children should be loved and cared for. This is where all teachings come from." — *Richie*
"Respect their elders, and value family and education." — *Kristin*

This makes me smile
"Being with family and friends." — *Richie*
"My husband, my dogs, wrestling, and 70's music." — *Kristin*

If you were stranded on a desert island, three things you would take with you
"My wife, a fishing pole, and sunscreen." — *Richie*
"My husband, a sailboat, and a radio." — *Kristin*

If you could leave one thing behind for the world to learn from life, it would be
"Take a chance, and don't be afraid to fail." — *Richie*
"Live life to its fullest potential, and always help others that are less fortunate." — *Kristin*

Our plans for the future are
"To have children, and build a ranch." — *Richie & Kristin*

My hero/heroes are
"There are many who have guided me throughout life." — *Richie*
"My father, Robert O'Leary." — *Kristin*

My favorite books/authors are
"*The Greatest Generation,* by Tom Brokaw." — *Richie*
"*Small Miracles,* by Yitta Halberstam and Judith Leventhal." — *Kristin*

First meal my spouse ever prepared for me
"Spaghetti." — *Richie*
"Seafood Gumbo." — *Kristin*

APPLE CRISP

5 apples, peeled, cored, and sliced
1 tablespoon water
1 tablespoon lemon juice
1¼ cups graham crackers, crushed

¼ cup brown sugar
¼ cup white sugar
1 teaspoon cinnamon
1 stick butter, melted

Preheat oven to 350 degrees. Arrange apple slices in a greased 8-inch baking pan. Sprinkle with water and lemon juice. Combine crushed graham crackers, sugars, cinnamon, and butter. Spread over apples; bake for 35 to 40 minutes.

Top with vanilla ice cream when served.

Favorite food/meal
"Steak and lobster." — *Richie*
"Lobster and ice cream." — *Kristin*

I wish I could sing like
"Van Morrison." — *Richie*
"Celine Dion." — *Kristin*

My friends call me (nickname)
"Richie." — *Richie*
"K.C." — *Kristin*

My ideal vacation
"Sail the Greek Islands." — *Richie*
"Warm weather, water, family, friends, and good food." — *Kristin*

Hobbies/Other Interests
"Golf, fishing, and sailing." — *Richie*
"Horseback riding, skiing, and running." — *Kristin*

I collect
"Portraits of historic events." — *Richie*

My wife, is special because
"She is very forgiving of my short comings. " — *Richie*

Opie (Jack Russell Terrier) and Kady (Black Lab).

My husband, is special because
"He is very caring and sensitive—he is an extremely hard worker, and he is a perfectionist at every thing he does." — *Kristin*

I am thankful my parents/ grandparents taught me
"The importance of family, a good education, and to accept all people of all kinds." — *Kristin*

99 *Nathan* DAVIS

DEFENSIVE LINEMAN • 6' 5" • 312

NFL EXPERIENCE
3rd year, Atlanta Falcons (1), Dallas Cowboys

BIRTHDAY
2-6-74

COLLEGE
Indiana

Nathan is the cousin of Barry Larkin, the perennial all-star shortstop with the Cincinnati Reds.

Chef Grady Spears's
CIDER ADOBO

³/₄ cup red wine
³/₄ cup apple cider vinegar
¹/₄ cup apricot preserves
¹/₄ cup honey
2 tablespoons packed brown sugar

1 teaspoon minced garlic
1 teaspoon, peeled and minced, fresh ginger
¹/₂ teaspoon kosher salt
1 scallion, thinly-cut on the diagonal
¹/₄ cup chopped cilantro leaves

Place all of the ingredients in a large, heavy pan; stir well, to combine. Place the pan over medium-high heat; bring the mixture to a boil, watching carefully so it does not boil over. Reduce heat to medium; cook the adobo, uncovered, stirring occasionally, until reduced by about 50 percent (to 1 cup). It will take 20 to 25 minutes to reduce. The consistency should be like syrup. Serve with the quail, or put the adobo into a jar to refrigerate, for future use. Adobo will keep about 5 days in the refrigerator.

Yield: 1 cup.

40

96 *Ebenezer* EKUBAN

DEFENSIVE LINEMAN • 6' 3" • 261

NFL EXPERIENCE
Rookie

BIRTHDAY
5-29-76

COLLEGE
North Carolina

Ebenezer is a native of Ghana, Africa.

If you could put your own message on a billboard for all to see, what would it be?
"Be blessed with what God has given you, because others are less fortunate."

All children should be taught to
"Value education, and respect their elders."

This makes me smile
"Having a positive impact on children' s lives."

If you were stranded on a desert island, three things you would take with you
"A family photo, a mirror, and a compass."

If you could leave one thing behind for the world to learn from life, it would be
"Enjoy life, because it goes by so fast."

My/Our plans for the future are
"To be happy at whatever I do, and to have a loving wife and family."

My hero/heroes are
"My parents."

Ebenezer Ekuban.

42

Chef Grady Spears's
COW TOWN COLESLAW

5 cups julienned green cabbage (about 1 head)
1 1/2 cups julienned red cabbage (about 1/3 head)
2 carrots, peeled and julienned
5 jalapeño peppers, stemmed, seeded, and
    julienned
1 1/4 cups mayonnaise

1/2 cup malt vinegar
1/2 cup sugar
1 1/2 tablespoons freshly-squeezed lime juice
kosher salt, to taste
freshly-ground pepper, to taste

Place all of the vegetables in a large bowl. In another bowl, whisk together the mayonnaise, vinegar, sugar, and lime juice. Pour the dressing over the vegetables, season with salt and pepper, and toss to combine. Set aside in the refrigerator, until serving time. It is best made and served on the same day.

Favorite food/meal

"Spinach stew with oxtail over white rice, geloff rice, and palm nut soup."

My friends call me (nickname)

"EB or E."

My ideal vacation

"A nice island get-away with a special someone."

Hobbies/Other Interests

"Charity work, and playing video games. I want to start learning how to golf."

I collect

"Sports cards, especially football cards."

When others describe you, what character qualities do they use?

"Humble, hard worker, sincere, and quiet."

My mother, is special because

"Not only did she bring me into the world, but she helped mold me to the person I am today."

If I were not playing football, I'd be a

"Physical therapist, or in real estate."

I am thankful my parents/ grandparents taught me

"That through God and hard work anything is possible, and to never run away from adversity."

Ebenezer was a pass rusher that the Cowboys could not pass up in the first round of the 1999 NFL Draft.

DEFENSIVE END • 6' 5" • 271

NFL EXPERIENCE
2nd year, Dallas Cowboys

BIRTHDAY
8-14-75 — *Greg*
5-8-75 — *Tangie*

COLLEGE
North Carolina — *Greg*

TANGIE'S OCCUPATION
Housewife

KIDS
Expecting January, 2000

Greg and Tangie on vacation in the Virgin Islands.

If you could put your own message on a billboard for all to see, what would it be?
"Jesus Christ loves you." — *Greg*
"Always be willing to lend a helping hand." — *Tangie*

All children should be taught to
"About God." — *Greg*
"To put God first, and respect their elders." — *Tangie*

This makes me smile
"Spending time with my wife." — *Greg*
"Spending time with my husband and my family." — *Tangie*

If you were stranded on a desert island, three things you would take with you
"Food that I could grow, water, and family." — *Greg*
"My husband, water, and my family." — *Tangie*

If you could leave one thing behind for the world to learn from life, it would be
"Love for one another." — *Greg*
"Always be kind, and respect people." — *Tangie*

Our plans for the future are
"To have a large family, and move back to North Carolina." — *Greg & Tangie*

My hero/heroes are
"Jesus." — *Greg & Tangie*

My favorite books/authors are
"The Bible." — *Greg*
"*Disappearing Acts*, by Terry McMillian." — *Tangie*

Chef Grady Spears's
CHAR-GRILLED SQUASH

2 zucchini squash
2 yellow squash
2 tablespoons olive oil

kosher salt, to taste
freshly-ground black pepper, to taste

Wash and dry the squash. Cut the root ends off, and slice the squash lengthwise in $1/2$-inch-thick slices. Lay the squash slices out on a plate; sprinkle them with oil, salt, and pepper. Place the slices on a very hot grill, and cook on both sides, until well done (about 10 minutes).

Yield: 4 servings.

First meal my spouse ever prepared for me
"Cubed steak with mashed potatoes and gravy." — *Greg*
"Pancakes and eggs." — *Tangie*

Favorite food/meal
"Pizza." — *Greg & Tangie*

I wish I could sing like
"Brian McKnight." — *Greg*
"Whitney Houston." —*Tangie*

My friends call me (nickname)
"Big Fella." — *Greg*

My ideal vacation
"A cruise." — *Greg & Tangie*

Hobbies/Other Interests
"Fishing." — *Greg*
"Reading, shopping, and listening to music." — *Tangie*

I collect
"Dolls." — *Tangie*

When others describe you, what character qualities do they use?
"Loving." — *Greg*
"Intelligent, kind, and giving." — *Tangie*

My wife, is special because
"I love her. " — *Greg*

My husband, is special because
"He is very caring and thoughtful." — *Tangie*

If I were not playing football, I'd be a
"High school teacher." — *Greg*

I am thankful my parents/ grandparents taught me
"About God." — *Greg*
"To always work hard." — *Tangie*

Greg having fun on vacation.

Ben FRICKE

NFL EXPERIENCE
1st year, Dallas Cowboys

BIRTHDAY
11-13-75

COLLEGE
Houston

PETS
Gabby - Dog

If you could put your own message on a billboard for all to see, what would it be?
"God loves you and has a plan for you."

All children should be taught to
"Respect the respectable."

This makes me smile
"Flying my airplane."

If you were stranded on a desert island, three things you would take with you
"The Bible, food, and water."

If you could leave one thing behind for the world to learn from life, it would be
"Perseverance, persistence, and faith will bring you your heart's desires."

My plans for the future are
"To own an NFL franchise."

My hero/heroes are
"Jesus Christ."

My favorite books/authors are
"The Bible, and many authors."

Favorite food/meal
"Roast, mashed potatoes, gravy, and red wine."

I wish I could sing like
"George Strait."

Ben Fricke—#69.

Chef Grady Spears's

CARAMELIZED BANANAS

³/₄ cup packed brown sugar
³/₄ cup cold unsalted butter, cut into pieces

4 bananas, diced

Heat the brown sugar in a skillet, over medium heat. When the sugar starts to melt, add the butter; stir, to blend, with a whisk or wooden spoon. When the mixture becomes liquid and very hot, add the bananas all at once. Stir, to coat the bananas with the syrup. Remove from heat; let cool. Serve the bananas at once, or store them the refrigerator for up to 2 days. Stir again before serving.

My friends call me (nickname)

"Frick."

My ideal vacation

"A trip to the moon."

Hobbies/Other Interests

"Flying, hunting, fishing, and reading."

I collect

"Guns."

When others describe you, what character qualities do they use?

"Serious, funny, analytical, political, goal-oriented, hard-working, and overachiever."

My mother, is special because

"She is very fun to be around, outgoing, and a professional."

If I were not playing football, I'd be a

"Finishing school, and applying for an MBA."

I am thankful my parents/grandparents taught me

"What it takes to achieve the goals you set for yourself."

NFL EXPERIENCE
9th year, New Orleans Saints
(1), Dallas Cowboys (8)

BIRTHDAY
3-28-66 — *Jason*
12-8-65 — *Brill*

COLLEGE
Princeton — *Jason*
Princeton and Harvard Law
School — *Brill*

BRILL'S OCCUPATION
Runs Jason Garrett
Starfish Charities

PETS
Maggie - Yellow
Labrador Retriever

Brill, Jason, and Maggie.

If you could put your own message on a billboard for all to see, what would it be?
"Take life one day at a time." — *Jason*
"Appreciate this day!" — *Brill*

All children should be taught to
"Believe in themselves." — *Jason*

This makes me smile
"Being with each other, family, and friends." — *Jason & Brill*

If you were stranded on a desert island, three things you would take with you
"Brill, Maggie, and music." — *Jason*
"Jason, Maggie, and books." — *Brill*

If you could leave one thing behind for the world to learn from life, it would be
"Life is short—smile, laugh, and have fun." — *Jason*
"To be kind to others." — *Brill*

Our plans for the future are
"To take life one day at a time." — *Jason & Brill*

My hero/heroes are
"My parents." — *Jason*

Brill and Jason with Jason's dad,
Jim Garrett, at training camp.

Chef Grady Spears's

REFRIGERATOR CHOCOLATE PIE WITH CARAMELIZED BANANAS

1 cup unsalted butter
1½ cups superfine granulated sugar
6 eggs
1½ tablespoons pure vanilla extract

2 teaspoons almond extract
1 cup sifted cocoa powder
1 prebaked 8-inch piecrust (page 36)
1 recipe Caramelized Bananas (page 47)

Cream the butter and sugar in a mixer fitted with a balloon whisk (or use a hand-held mixer), until light in color and texture. Add the eggs, one at a time, beating well after each addition. Blend in the extracts; sift the cocoa over the creamed mixture. Set the mixer speed on medium-low; beat for 30 minutes. The mixture will be light and an intense chocolate color. Pour or scrape the mixture into the piecrust; refrigerate the pie for 24 hours before serving. If you cover it with plastic wrap, it will leave marks on the top of the pie; it is better to leave the pie uncovered, or cover with some-thing that will not touch the surface. Serve with the Caramelized Bananas.

Yield: 6 servings.

My favorite books/authors are
"*Nine Stories,* by J.D. Salinger." — *Jason*
"*Great Gatsby,* by F. Scott Fitzgerald; *Crossing to Safety,* by Wallace Steyner." — *Brill*

First meal my spouse ever prepared for me
"Tacos." — *Jason*
"Delicious eggs." — *Brill*

Favorite food/meal
"Turkey dinner." — *Jason*
"Beef tenderloin (cooked by my dad), French fries, and nachos." — *Brill*

I wish I could sing like
"Frank Sinatra." — *Jason*
"Diana Ross." — *Brill*

My friends call me (nickname)
"Red, and Red Ball." — *Jason*
"Brillo, and Brillster." — *Brill*

Daryl Johnston, Jason, and Mark Tuinei.

My ideal vacation
"Going to the beach!" — *Jason & Brill*

Hobbies/Other Interests
"Movies and a little golf." — *Jason*
"Reading and movies." — *Brill*

My wife, is special because
"She is extremely thoughtful and kind." — *Jason*

My husband, is special because
"It is always important to him to do his best to be a good person." — *Brill*

I am thankful my parents/grandparents taught me
"The importance of family." — *Jason*
"To be honest." — *Brill*

56 *Randall* GODFREY

LINEBACKER • 6' 2" • 245

NFL EXPERIENCE
4th year, Dallas Cowboys

BIRTHDAY
4-6-73

COLLEGE
Georgia

PETS
Buddy & Killer - Miniature
Doberman Pinchers

All children should be taught to
"Respect adults."

My plans for the future are
"To get married, and to have a family."

My hero/heroes are
"My parents."

My favorite books/authors are
"Charles Haley's book."

Favorite food/meal
"Greens, corn bread, BBQ chicken, and black-eyed peas."

I wish I could sing like
"Luther Vandross."

My friends call me (nickname)
"Zeus."

My ideal vacation
"Bahamas—with my girlfriend."

Hobbies/Other Interests
"Fishing, hunting, bike riding, and PlayStation."

I collect
"Football cards, and autographed pictures of NFL players."

Godfrey's physical and active style of play fits the Cowboys defensive scheme.

Chef Grady Spears's
RED CHILE PASTE

4 ancho chiles	3 cups chicken stock
4 New Mexican dried chiles, or Mexican guajillos	$1/2$ white onion, diced
	3 cloves garlic, minced

Slit each chile with a sharp knife; remove the seeds and stem.

Place the peppers in a large saucepan; cover them with the chicken stock. Add the onion and garlic. Bring the stock to a boil, over high heat; reduce heat, and allow to simmer for about 15 minutes, or until the peppers have absorbed some liquid and have become soft. Pour the pepper mixture and cooking liquid into a blender. Blend, on low speed, increasing to high speed as the purée combines.

My mother and grandmother, are special because

"They brought me up in a way that I respect others."

If I were not playing football, I'd be a

"Coach."

Randall Godrey—#56.

4 GOWIN

NFL EXPERIENCE
3rd year, Dallas Cowboys

BIRTHDAY
3-30-75 — *Toby*
10-24-74 — *Niki*

COLLEGE
North Texas — *Toby*

NIKI'S OCCUPATION
Massage Therapist

PETS
Dallas and Madison -
Miniature Schnauzers

Toby and Niki enjoying dinner on vacation.

If you could put your own message on a billboard for all to see, what would it be?
"True wealth is what you are, not what you have." — *Toby & Niki*

All children should be taught to
"Set goals, challenge themselves, and achieve them." — *Toby & Niki*

This makes me smile
"Watching my husband fulfill his dreams." — *Niki*

If you were stranded on a desert island, three things you would take with you
"Food, water, and family." — *Toby*
"My husband and two dogs, Dallas and Madison." — *Niki*

If you could leave one thing behind for the world to learn from life, it would be
"Our family picture album, because it shows family bonding, and that's something I believe our world is lacking." — *Toby & Niki*

Our plans for the future are
"To be blessed with children, and make every moment count." — *Toby & Niki*

First meal my spouse ever prepared for me
"Chicken Parmesan." — *Toby*
"Grilled steak and shrimp k-bobs— he's a great cook." — *Niki*

Favorite food/meal
"Seafood pasta, or a good steak." — *Toby*
"Stuffed filet and rosemary new potatoes from my favorite chef, Rob Gowin, at Sadler's Kitchen in Jacksonville, Texas." — *Niki*

I wish I could sing like
"I just wish I could carry a tune." — *Niki*

My friends call me (nickname)
"The Toe." — *Toby*
"Angie." — *Niki*

TEXAS TRASH

4 cups Cheerios	2¹/₂ sticks butter
4 cups Wheat Chex	2 teaspoons Nature's Seasoning
4 cups Rice Chex	1 teaspoon garlic salt
4 cups Corn Chex	1 teaspoon celery salt
4 cups Crispix	1 teaspoon cayenne pepper
1 box stick pretzels	7 tablespoons Worcestershire sauce
pecans, optional	12 dashes Tabasco

Place all cereals, pretzels, and pecans in a large bowl. Melt together butter and all seasonings. Pour butter mixture over cereal; mix well. Bake on a cookie sheet at 250 degrees for 1¹/₂ hours. Stir every 20 minutes.

CARPENTER'S JELLO DELIGHT

1 small package orange Jello	2 small cans mandarin oranges
8 ounces sour cream	2 small cans pineapple tidbits
8 ounces Cool Whip	

Sprinkle dry Jello mix over sour cream; mix well. Fold in Cool Whip, mandarin oranges, and pineapple. Chill.
This recipe was given to Niki by her sister and brother-in-law, Kelli and Kevin Carpenter.

My ideal vacation

"A week in the tropics to enjoy snorkeling and the beach; then, a week in the mountains to enjoy fishing, river rafting, etc.—the best of both worlds." — *Toby & Niki*

Hobbies/Other Interests

"Fishing, hunting, and playing golf." — *Toby*
"Exercising, painting, and cooking." — *Niki*

When others describe you, what character qualities do they use?

"Humble, very driven, and hard working." — *Toby*
"Focused, creative, and giving." — *Niki*

Our pride and joy—Madison and Dallas.

My wife, is special because
"She is very supportive, loving, and encouraging." — *Toby*

My husband, is special because
"He is everything to me. I believe he is truly a blessing." — *Niki*

Toby's favorite pasttime—fishing for bass on Lake Ray Roberts

54 *Darren* HAMBRICK

LINEBACKER • 6' 2" • 227

NFL EXPERIENCE
2nd year, Dallas Cowboys

BIRTHDAY
8-30-75

COLLEGE
South Carolina

KIDS
Darren, Jr. (5)

PETS
Dog

If you could put your own message on a billboard for all to see, what would it be?
"D' Ham Alert."

All children should be taught to
"Respect."

This makes me smile
"To win a game."

If you were stranded on a desert island, three things you would take with you
"Food, water, and fire flames."

If you could leave one thing behind for the world to learn from life, it would be
"To live one day at a time."

My/Our plans for the future are
"To be financially successful."

My hero/heroes are
"Deion Sanders and Michael Irvin."

My favorite books/authors are
"Steven King."

Favorite food/meal
"Pork chops, rice, and corn."

I wish I could sing like
"R. Kelly."

My friends call me (nickname)
"D' Ham."

My ideal vacation
"Bahamas."

Hobbies/Other Interests
"Fishing and hunting."

I collect
"Hats."

Hambrick finished last season second on the team in special team tackles.

Chef Grady Spears's

JALAPEÑO JELLY

12 jalapeño peppers, stemmed and seeded   6 cups sugar
1½ cups cider vinegar   6 ounces liquid fruit pectin

If you have sensitive skin, wear gloves when handling the hot peppers.

Place the jalapeños in a blender. Pour the vinegar over them; blend to purée the peppers. Transfer the pepper liquid to a large saucepan; add the sugar. Stir together, and bring to a boil, over medium heat. Continue to cook; stir for 5 minutes, or until the sugar dissolves. Remove the liquid from the heat; let it cool for 10 minutes. At that time, blend the pectin into the jalapeño mixture.

Remove any foam from the top of the jelly with a spoon. Pour the jelly into 8-ounce jars. Put lids on the jars, and store until needed.

When others describe you, what character qualities do they use?
"Funny."

MyMother and grandmother, is special because
"They raised me up to what I am, and they will always believe in me."

If I were not playing football, I'd be a
"Businessman."

I am thankful my parents/ grandparents taught me
"Right from wrong."

Darren Hambrick high jumped 7'1¾" in the Florida state track meet his senior year in high school.

38

Duane HAWTHORNE

DEFENSIVE BACK • 5' 10" • 165

NFL EXPERIENCE
Rookie

BIRTHDAY
8-26-76

COLLEGE
Northern Illinois

Duane was team MVP All-Suburban East Conference, all-district,
and all-metro, as a senior at Ladue High School in St. Louis, Missouri.

Chef Grady Spears's
CAJETA SAUCE (CARAMEL SAUCE)

4 cups sugar
1 cup water

1 to 2 cups heavy cream, or fresh goat's milk
¼ cup unsalted butter

Combine the sugar and water in a large, wide, heavy saucepan; bring it to a boil. Use a pan in which you can see the color of the sugar as it cooks. Stir, as needed, to dissolve sugar. Do not stir again once the mixture begins to simmer. Continue a steady boil, to reduce the mixture; bring it to a light brown color. This may take 20 to 30 minutes. When the light brown color is reached, watch carefully as it changes to golden brown. It should be fairly thick. At this moment, remove it from the heat; slowly stir the butter into the sugar syrup. Blend in enough cream to make the consistency fairly thick, yet still golden brown in color.

As sauce cools, it becomes thicker. Serve cajeta warm. Store any extra in the refrigerator.

Yield: approximately 4 cups.

56

"Children Today – Adults Tomorrow"

SIEMENS

Siemens is proud to partner with the
Dallas Cowboys Courage House at Happy Hill Farm
to give boys and girls the second chance
in life that they deserve.

http://www.usa.siemens.com/

Dale & Brooke
HELLESTRAE

OFFENSIVE LINEMAN • 6' 5" • 291

NFL EXPERIENCE
15th year, Buffalo Bills (4),
Los Angeles Raiders (1),
Dallas Cowboys (10)

BIRTHDAY
7-11-62 — *Dale*
11-28-63 — *Brooke*

COLLEGE
SMU — *Dale*
Phoenix College — *Brooke*

BROOKE'S OCCUPATION
Wife, mom, and co-owner
with Dale of two
"Cookies by Design"
in Arizona

KIDS
Hillary (7), Kendyll (4)

Brooke, Hillary, Dale, and Kendyll in Salsburg.

If you could put your own message on a billboard for all to see, what would it be?
"Cookies are Healthy—buy your cookies from 'Cookies by Design'—(480) 991-2737." — *Dale*
"What positive difference have you made for someone today?" — *Brooke*

All children should be taught to
"Value their family, friends, and the value of an education." — *Dale*
"How important it is to have a big heart toward other people." — *Brooke*

This makes me smile
"My family, and friends." — *Dale*
"When I count all the intangible blessings in my life." — *Brooke*

If you were stranded on a desert island, three things you would take with you
"My family, golf clubs, and Mountain Dew." — *Dale*
"Dale, Hillary, and Kendyll." — *Brooke*

If you could leave one thing behind for the world to learn from life, it would be
"Treat people the way you would like to be treated." — *Dale*
"Love people—not possessions." — *Brooke*

Our plans for the future are
"To make a positive impact on people's lives." — *Dale & Brooke*

Hillary and Kendyll Hellestrae.

CHEESY CHICKEN

6 boneless, skinless chicken breasts
6 slices Swiss cheese
2 cans cream of chicken soup
¼ cup cooking sherry

¼ cup milk
2 cups Pepperidge Farm Herb Stuffing, uncooked
½ cup margarine or butter, melted

In a small bowl, mix soup, cooking sherry, and milk. In another bowl, mix stuffing with melted margarine.

Place chicken breasts flat in a 9x13-inch glass baking dish. Place one slice of cheese on top of each piece of chicken. Once they're all covered, pour the soup mixture on top; spread it evenly, so all of the cheese is covered. Next, spread the stuffing on top, covering it evenly.

Cover the baking dish with foil; cook at 350 degrees for 1 hour. Remove foil; cook 10 more minutes, to brown the stuffing.

This is not "low fat," but it's yummy!

My hero/heroes are
"Walt Frazier and Billy Joe Dupree." — *Dale*
"Dale is my hero." — *Brooke*

My favorite books/authors are
"John Grisham." — *Dale*
"Elizabeth George books, Gene Edwards, C.S. Lewis, and The Bible." — *Brooke*

First meal my spouse ever prepared for me
"Breakfast in bed, when we got home from our honeymoon." — *Brooke*

My mother, is special because
"She makes everyone around her happy and makes them better people." — *Dale*

My mother, is special because
"She is a perfect example and my best girlfriend." — *Brooke*

Favorite food/meal
"My wife's beef stroganoff." — *Dale*
"Ice cream." — *Brooke*

I wish I could sing like
"Garth Brooks." — *Dale*
"Celine Dion." — *Brooke*

The Hellestraes "on top of the world" in Austria.

Dale and Brooke in the mountains of Telluride, Colorado.

My friends call me (nickname)
"Strapper, Helle." — *Dale*
"Brooker." — *Brooke*

If I were not playing football, I'd be a
"High school teacher and coach." — *Dale*

Nate HEMSLEY

LINEBACKER • 6' 0" • 228

NFL EXPERIENCE
2nd year, Dallas Cowboys

BIRTHDAY
5-15-74

COLLEGE
Syracuse

PETS
Smoke - Cat;
Blaze - Dog

If you could put your own message on a billboard for all to see, what would it be?
"Peace."

All children should be taught to
"Respect their elders."

This makes me smile
"Courtney (girlfriend)."

If you could leave one thing behind for the world to learn from life, it would be
"The knowledge from all my mistakes."

My plans for the future are
"Get married, and have a family."

My hero/heroes are
"My mother."

Favorite food/meal
"Philly cheesesteak ."

I wish I could sing like
"Barry White."

My ideal vacation
"Relaxing in a house on a beach in St. Thomas with Courtney."

Hobbies/Other Interests
"PlayStation."

I collect
"CDs."

When others describe you, what character qualities do they use?
"Friendly and outgoing."

My mother, is special because
"Of her strength."

Courtney and Nate visiting Syracuse University.

Chef Grady Spears's

GARLIC MASHED POTATOES

2 pounds russet potatoes
15 cloves garlic, peeled
5 tablespoons unsalted butter

³/₄ cup heavy cream
kosher salt, to taste
freshly-ground pepper, to taste

Peel potatoes; cut them into 1¹/₂-inch thick pieces. Place the pieces in a large, heavy saucepan, along with the garlic cloves; cover the potatoes with 1 inch of cold water. Place the saucepan on high heat, and bring the water to a boil. Turn the heat down to medium, cover the pot, and cook the potatoes, until they are just soft when tested with the tip of a knife, about 20 minutes.

While the potatoes are cooking, heat the butter and cream in another saucepan. Reduce by one- fourth.

When potatoes and garlic are cooked, drain them. Mash the potatoes and garlic, while pouring in the hot cream mixture. Stir the salt and pepper into the finished potatoes. Serve at once, or place the covered bowl over another pan of simmering water, to keep warm.

If I were not playing football, I'd be a
"Working in the business marketing field."

I am thankful my parents/grandparents taught me
"Responsibility."

Nate's mother at Nate and Courtney's house.

Chad & Tammy HENNINGS

DEFENSIVE LINEMAN • 6' 6" • 291

NFL EXPERIENCE
8th year, Dallas Cowboys

BIRTHDAY
10-20-65 — *Chad*
12-11-66 — *Tammy*

COLLEGE
Air Force Academy — *Chad*

TAMMY'S OCCUPATION
Homemaker

KIDS
Chase (6), Brenna (2)

Chad, Chase, Tammy, and Brenna on a lake in Iowa.

If you could put your own message on a billboard for all to see, what would it be?
"Humble yourself before the Lord!" — *Chad*
"You know Jesus?" — *Tammy*

All children should be taught to
"Be accountable for their actions, and to respect themselves." — *Chad*
"Know right from wrong, and always make the right decisions." — *Tammy*

This makes me smile
"Spending time with my family." — *Chad*
"When my family is happy, and when I see my kids make good choices." — *Tammy*

First meal my spouse ever prepared for me
"Lasagna." — *Chad*
"Chef-Boy-R-Dee pizza." — *Tammy*

If you were stranded on a desert island, three things you would take with you
"Bible, pictures of my family, and my wife." — *Chad*
"Bible, loved ones, and—that's all." — *Tammy*

If you could leave one thing behind for the world to learn from life, it would be
"Take care of what God gave us." — *Tammy*

Our plans for the future are
"To raise our children to be upstanding, moral, Christian adults." — *Chad & Tammy*

My hero/heroes are
"John Wayne, and my father." — *Chad*

My favorite books/authors are
"'Left Behind' series." — *Chad*
"Author of any good book." — *Tammy*

Chad and his brother, Todd, boating in Iowa.

GERMAN POTATO SALAD

6 potatoes	1½ teaspoons salt
6 slices bacon	½ to 1 teaspoon celery seed
¾ cup onion, chopped	pinch of pepper
2 tablespoons flour	¾ cup water
2 teaspoons sugar	½ cup vinegar

Boil and slice potatoes; leave on the skins.

Fry bacon, until crisp; drain. In bacon grease, sauté onion. Mix in flour, sugar, salt, celery seed, and pepper. Blend into sautéed onion; cook, until smooth. Add water and vinegar to onion mixture. Boil for 1 minute.

Pour over potato and crushed bacon; mix. Let marinate a while in refrigerator. Can heat before serving, or eat cold. Makes 6-8 servings.

Best potato salad ever! This recipe is from Chad's grandmother.

AUNT MARILYN'S RED RASPBERRY PARFAIT

1 small carton whipping cream	1 cup powdered sugar
1 8-ounce package cream cheese	2 packages frozen red raspberries, thawed

Whip cream in a small bowl; whip cream cheese in another bowl. Fold together; add powdered sugar. Alternate layers of cream mixture and berries in pretty bowls or glasses.

Favorite food/meal

"Pizza and steak." — *Chad*

"Mexican—and hot!" — *Tammy*

I wish I could sing like

"Tom Jones." — *Chad*

"Jaci Valasquez and Barbra Streisand." — *Tammy*

My friends call me (nickname)

"Hans." — *Chad*

"Tam." — *Tammy*

My ideal vacation

"Colorado on horseback." — *Chad*

"Anywhere there is cold mountain air!" — *Tammy*

Chase, Brenna, and Chad swimming.

Hobbies/Other Interests

"Reading, Bible study, watch movies (old ones), public speaking, and current events." — *Chad*

"Golfing, reading, nutrition, alternative medicine, and mountains." — *Tammy*

I collect

"John Wayne movies." — *Chad*

When others describe you, what character qualities do they use?

"Honorable." — *Chad*

My wife, is special because

"She's always herself, and she keeps me grounded." — *Chad*

My husband, is special because

"He is so committed and faithful to what he believes in." — *Tammy*

66 *Tony* HUTSON

GUARD • 6' 3" • 306

NFL EXPERIENCE
3rd year, Dallas Cowboys

BIRTHDAY
3-13-74

COLLEGE
Northeastern State (Okla.)

All children should be taught to
"Respect people."

My plans for the future are
"To be happy."

My hero/heroes are
"My father."

My favorite books/authors are
"Cat in the Hat."

Favorite food/meal
"All."

My friends call me (nickname)
"T-Hut."

Hobbies/Other Interests
"Fishing."

My mother, is special because
"She is my heart."

If I were not playing football, I'd be a
"Couch potato."

Through hard work and perseverance, Tony has reached the point where he has become a valuable and versatile member of the offensive liine.

Chef Grady Spears's REATA GRILL BLEND

4 tablespoons kosher salt
3 tablespoons Pasilla Powder (page 142)
2 tablespoons dried granulated garlic
2 tablespoons sugar

2 tablespoons ground cumin
2 tablespoons coarsely-ground black pepper
1 tablespoon ground thyme

Combine all of the ingredients in a small bowl, blending well, to evenly distribute the spices. Be sure to break up any chunks that appear. Store the blend in an airtight container. Shake or stir it again before each use.

Yield: about 1 cup.

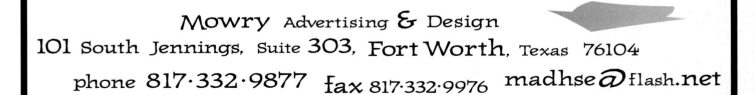

Michael & Sandy
IRVIN

ALL-PRO WIDE RECEIVER • 6' 2" • 207

NFL EXPERIENCE
12th year, Dallas Cowboys

BIRTHDAY
3-5-66 — *Michael*
1-2-66 — *Sandy*

COLLEGE
Miami (FL) — *Michael*

SANDY'S OCCUPATION
Housewife and mother

KIDS
Myesha (9), Chelsea (4),
Michael, II (2), Elijah (1)

Elijah and Michael, II.

All children should be taught to
"Love their parents." — *Michael*
"Obey your parents and respect your elders." — *Sandy*

My plans for the future are
"God's will." — *Michael*

My hero/heroes are
"My father was my hero." — *Michael*
"My husband, Michael Irvin." — *Sandy*

My favorite books/authors are
"The Bible." — *Michael*
"The Holy Bible." — *Sandy*

First meal my spouse ever prepared for me
"Chicken and dressing." — *Michael*
"Cabbage, macaroni and cheese, and country ice tea." — *Sandy*

Favorite food/meal
"Seafood." — *Michael & Sandy*

I wish I could sing like
"Al Green." — *Michael*
"Patti LaBelle." — *Sandy*

My friends call me (nickname)
"Play Maker." — *Michael*

Myesha, Chelsea, and Michael with Rowdy
at Texas Stadium Cowboys family room.

SANDY'S JAZZY JAMBALAYA

8 ounces hot turkey-sausage links, andouille or
kielbasa, cut into ¹/₄-inch-thick rounds
1 medium-size yellow onion, chopped
1 medium-size celery stalk, diced
1 garlic clove, minced
¹/₈ teaspoon cayenne pepper
1¹/₂ cups regular long-grain rice
1¹/₂ teaspoons chopped fresh, or ¹/₂ teaspoon,
dried thyme

¹/₂ teaspoon turmeric
¹/₂ teaspoon salt, optional
14-ounce can reduced-sodium chicken broth
16-ounce can tomatoes, drained and chopped
1 cup frozen green peas, thawed
¹/₂ pound medium-size shrimp, shelled, and
deveined; if desired, halve lengthwise, to
stretch
sprigs of thyme, optional garnish

Cook sausage, in 5-quart Dutch oven, over low heat, to render fat; increase heat, to medium-high, and cook, until browned. Remove sausage.

Add onion and celery to drippings in pot; cook about 5 minutes. Add garlic and cayenne; cook, stirring, every 30 seconds. Add rice; cook, stirring for 1 minute. Stir in thyme, turmeric, salt (if desired) and broth with enough water added to it to equal 3 cups.

Return sausage to pot; heat to boiling, over high heat. Reduce heat, to low; cover, and cook 15 minutes. Stir in tomatoes with juice and peas; cover, and cook 5 minutes. Stir in shrimp; cover, and cook until shrimp turn opaque throughout, about 5 additional minutes. Spoon jambalaya into serving bowls; garnish with thyme. Serve with hot-pepper sauce, if desired.

Yield: 6 servings.

My ideal vacation

"Disney World
with our kids." — *Michael & Sandy*

Hobbies/Other Interests

"Shooting pool." — *Michael*

"Shopping and traveling." — *Sandy*

I collect

"Super Bowl rings." — *Michael*

"Thomas Blackshear's Ebony Visions,
and Florence Originals
Giuseppe Armani." — *Sandy*

Michael and Michael, II—
at his first hockey game.

Sandy and Michael at the
Atlantis Paradise Island Resort
in the Bahamas celebrating
their ninth wedding
anniversary—June, 1999.

My wife, is special because
"She knows her love for
me is heaven sent."
— *Michael*

67

81

Raghib & Melani ISMAIL

WIDE RECEIVER • 5′ 11″ • 175

NFL EXPERIENCE
7th year, Raiders (3), Carolina Panthers (3), Dallas Cowboys

BIRTHDAY
11-18-69 — *Raghib*

COLLEGE
Notre Dame — *Raghib*

KIDS
Noe (3), Imani (2)

My friends call me (nickname)
"Rocket." — *Raghib*

Rocket's speed will add a vertical dimension to the Cowboys passing game.

Chef Grady Spears's CRACKED-PEPPER GRAVY

¹/₄ cup unsalted butter
5 tablespoons flour
2¹/₂ cups milk

1¹/₂ teaspoons kosher salt
4 teaspoons cracked pepper

Melt the butter in a heavy saucepan. When the foam goes down, whisk in the flour. Continually whisk, until the flour cooks, becoming a fragrant light brown. Slowly add the milk, continuing to whisk, to keep lumps from forming. Season with salt and pepper. Simmer gravy for 10 minutes, to cook and reduce. Serve hot.

Sept 7, 1999 *From the desk of David McDavid*

To all Dallas Cowboy Fans:

At the David McDavid Auto Group, we are proud to support the Happy Hill Farm Academy and Home. The Happy Hill Farm helps children with a broad range of behavioral and academic problems, who are many times victims of abuse or neglect. For whatever reason, these children are unable to live and study in more traditional family and community settings. At Happy Hill Farm, these children are given another chance to make a better life for themselves.

I want to express appreciation to the Dallas Cowboys for their support of the Dallas Cowboys Courage House at Happy Hill Farm Academy/ Home. The Courage House is making a difference in the lives of troubled, needy kids.

The program at Happy Hill Farm is operated mostly with contributions from friends, foundations, corporations and organizations. The Farm receives no state, federal or local tax funding, so we need your help. Join me, the David McDavid Auto Group, and The Dallas Cowboys in helping secure the future for these children. You could be providing a second chance for a young Texan.

Happy Hill Farm is a non-profit, charitable, tax-exempt Texas corporation, so your generous gift will be fully tax-deductible. Please call or write Happy Hill Farm Academy and Home at HC 51 Box 56 Granbury, TX 76048 (254) 897-4822.

Thank you for your generosity,

David McDavid
Chairman, The David McDavid Auto Group
Boardmember, Happy Hill Farm Academy/Home

A Proud Sponsor
THE DALLAS
COWBOYS
COURAGE HOUSE
AT HAPPY HILL FARM

Happy Hill Farm Academy/Home
HC51 • Box 56 Granbury, TX 76048 254-897-4822

Daryl & Diane
JOHNSTON

ALL-PRO RUNNING BACK • 6' 2" • 242

NFL EXPERIENCE
11th year, Dallas Cowboys

BIRTHDAY
2-10-66 — *Daryl*
10-22-67 — *Diane*

COLLEGE
Syracuse — *Daryl*

DIANE'S OCCUPATION
Kim Dawson Model

PETS
Otis - Golden Retriever

Daryl and Diane.

If you were stranded on a desert island, three things you would take with you

"My wife, a good book, and a cell phone—just in case we wanted to leave." — *Daryl*

"My husband, food, and a large boat— so we could leave!" — *Diane*

My hero/heroes are

"My parents." — *Daryl*

"My caring and loving husband." — *Diane*

If you could leave one thing behind for the world to learn from life, it would be

"Relentless pursuit of your dreams and ambitions." — *Daryl*

"Life is really too short— live everyday to the fullest." — *Diane*

Our plans for the future are

"To raise a family and grow old together." — *Daryl & Diane*

If you could put your own message on a billboard for all to see, what would it be?

"Failure to try is the only true failure." — *Daryl*

"'Do unto others as you would have done unto you.'" — *Diane*

All children should be taught to

"Give their best effort in all their endeavors." — *Daryl*

"Be responsible for their actions." — *Diane*

This makes me smile

"Andy Griffith show." — *Daryl*

"My dog." — *Diane*

Daryl, Mark Stepnoski, and Mark Tuinei with Brad Whitford and Joey Kramer of Aerosmith.

COLD CUCUMBER SALAD

6 cucumbers, peeled	$^1/_2$ cup vinegar
1 bunch of green onions, chopped	1 cup water
$^1/_2$ cup sugar	freshly-cracked pepper, to taste

Slice cucumbers into a large bowl, using a grater. *(It's quicker, easier, and slices the cucumbers thinner than slicing with a knife.)*

Add the rest of the ingredients; chill, and serve. Salad tastes best if made 2 to 3 hours ahead of time.

My favorite books/authors are

"Tom Clancy, and conspiracy theory books." — *Daryl*

"I love to read most anything on the bestseller list." — *Diane*

First meal my spouse ever prepared for me

"Shrimp and scallop stir-fry with vegetables." — *Daryl*

"Marinated, grilled vegetables." — *Diane*

Favorite food/meal

"A Del Frisco's steak, and skillet potatoes." — *Daryl*

"Too many to name." — *Diane*

I wish I could sing like

"Bono from U2." — *Daryl*

"I just wish I could sing!" — *Diane*

My friends call me (nickname)

"D. J." — *Daryl*

If I were not playing football, I'd be a

"Enjoying longer summer vacations." — *Daryl*

My ideal vacation

"Any setting that inspires relaxation with my wife." — *Daryl*

"Somewhere quiet with my husband." — *Diane*

Hobbies/Other Interests

"Golfing." — *Daryl*

"Reading, exercise, cooking, and travel." — *Diane*

I collect

"Sports memorabilia." — *Daryl*

"Limoges boxes." — *Diane*

Daryl, Eric Bjornson, and Jason Garrett with Santa.

When others describe you, what character qualities do they use?

"Strong work ethic, and considerate about others." — *Daryl*

"I don't know—you'd have to ask other people—I just hope it's positive." — *Diane*

My wife, is special because

"She is always there for me—through good times and bad times—supporting my decisions." — *Daryl*

My husband, is special because

"He is able to give so much to others and still balance his career, family, and friends." — *Diane*

I am thankful my parents/ grandparents taught me

"Do things the right way, be respectful of those people around me, and be responsible for my actions." — *Daryl*

71

Mike & Kimberly KISELAK

GUARD • 6' 3" • 295

NFL EXPERIENCE
2nd year, Dallas Cowboys

BIRTHDAY
3-9-67 — *Mike*
11-30-66 — *Kimberly*

COLLEGE
Maryland — *Mike*

KIMBERLY'S OCCUPATION
Southwest Airlines—Customer Care Representative

KIDS
Expecting first child February, 2000

PETS
Crunch - German Shepherd

Kimberly and Michael in Antigua, after football season in February—our honeymoon after 7 years.

If you could put your own message on a billboard for all to see, what would it be?

"Look to God, the rest comes into focus— Signed: Someone who knows." — *Mike*

All children should be taught to

"Believe that they are the best they know, but they are no better than you." — *Mike*
"Love one another." — *Kimberly*

This makes me smile

"Winning." — *Mike*
"My husband." — *Kimberly*

If you were stranded on a desert island, three things you would take with you

"My Bible, my wife, and my baby-to-be." — *Mike*

If you could leave one thing behind for the world to learn from life, it would be

"A statement saying: It's where you end up, not where you start." — *Mike*
"Trust in God." — *Kimberly*

My plans for the future are

"Build a strong family, and preach the Gospel to whoever has ears to hear, and, of course, play football for as long as the Lord allows me." — *Mike*
"To raise our family." — *Kimberly*

When others describe you, what character qualities do they use?

"I hope—faithful." — *Mike*
"Dependable, caring." — *Kimberly*

'Da Boys—Crunch and Samson, relaxing.

Chef Grady Spears's

APPLE CRISP WITH CAJETA

8 Granny Smith apples, peeled and cored
1 cup heavy cream
$^1/_2$ cup sugar
$^1/_4$ cup flour
1 tablespoon ground cinnamon
1 tablespoon freshly-squeezed lemon juice
$^1/_2$ teaspoon kosher salt

TOPPING
$1^1/_2$ cups flour
1 cup packed light brown sugar
2 teaspoons ground cinnamon
$^1/_4$ teaspoon kosher salt
12 tablespoons unsalted butter
Cajeta Sauce (page 56)

Butter a 9 by 13-inch pan. Slice the apples into thin wedges. Toss the apple slices in a large bowl with the cream, sugar, flour, cinnamon, lemon juice, and salt. Layer the apples into the prepared pan. Preheat oven to 350 degrees.

TOPPING: Mix the flour, brown sugar, cinnamon, and salt in a bowl. Cut the cold butter into small pieces; blend it with the dry mixture, using a fork or your hands. The mixture should not be over-worked. It will look crumbly. Spread the topping over the apples.

Bake for 45 minutes to 1 hour, or until the apples are soft and mixture is bubbling. Serve warm with Cajeta Sauce drizzled on top.

Yield: 8 servings.

My hero/heroes are

"Jesus Christ." — *Mike*

My favorite books/authors are

"The Bible, and all the authors." — *Mike*

First meal my spouse ever prepared for me

"Barbecued chicken and rice." — *Mike*
"Steak dinner." — *Kimberly*

Favorite food/meal

"Veal parmesan and chicken paprikash (see 1998 Cookbook)." — *Mike*
"Stuffed cabbage." — *Kimberly*

My ideal vacation

"White sand, blue sky, bright sun, clear water, ocean breeze, sun block on my face, and a drink in my hand." — *Mike*

Hobbies/Other Interests

"Sharing the Gospel, dining at nice restaurants, and seeing the world." — *Mike*

My wife, mother, and grandmother, are special because

"My wife, because she is a Psalms 31 woman. My mother, because she always put her children before herself. My grandmother, because life was and is tough at times for her. She never gives up. " — *Mike*

My mother, is special because

"She is always there for me." — *Kimberly*

If I were not playing football, I'd be a

"Minister and serve the Lord some way." — *Mike*

Michael with sister-in-law—Michelle, and two nieces—
Kara and Jordan, in Dallas for summer vacation (June, 1999).

NFL EXPERIENCE
3rd year, Dallas Cowboys

BIRTHDAY
1-29-74 — *David*
12-20-73 — *Melody*

COLLEGE
Louisiana State — *David*
McNeese State — *Melody*

PETS
Duke - Black Lab

David, Melody, Rene Story, Eric Bjornson, and Niki and Toby Gowin at an Aerosmith concert (April, 1999).

If you could put your own message on a billboard for all to see, what would it be?
"For people to just be more courteous to one another." — *Melody*

All children should be taught to
"Respect others, and treat others only as they themselves would like to be treated." — *David & Melody*

This makes me smile
"Being back in Louisiana with friends and family." — *David*
"To be with my husband and family." — *Melody*

Our plans for the future are
"To eventually move back to Louisiana and raise a family." — *David & Melody*

My hero is
"My dad." — *David*

My favorite books/authors are
"Favorite author: Tom Clancy. Favorite book: *Without Remorse*." — *David*
"No specific author. I love any good mystery." — *Melody*

Favorite food/meal
"Gumbo." — *David & Melody*

I wish I could sing like
"George Strait." — *David*
"Celine Dion." — *Melody*

My friends call me (nickname)
"Daddy." — *David*
"Mel." — *Melody*

My ideal vacation
"Anywhere I can enjoy the outdoors." — *David*
"Boca Raton, Florida—it is where my grandpa lived and my family went every summer when I was growing up. It definitely would hold the most memories." — *Melody*

Hobbies/Other Interests
"Hunting and fishing." — *David*
"Anything outdoors—running, bike riding, walking with friends—and reading." — *Melody*

JAMBALAYA

2 pounds pork, cubed
1 pound smoked sausage, sliced
1/4 cup shortening, or bacon drippings
2 cups onions, chopped
2 cups celery, chopped
1/4 cup garlic, diced
7 cups beef or chicken stock

2 cups mushrooms, sliced
1 cup green onions, sliced
1/4 cup parsley, chopped
salt and cayenne pepper, to taste
dash of hot sauce
4 cups rice

In a two-gallon Dutch oven, heat shortening, or bacon drippings, over medium-high heat. Sauté cubed pork, until dark on all sides and some pieces are sticking to the bottom of the pot (approximately 30 minutes). Add sausage; stir fry an additional 10 to 15 minutes. Tilt pot; ladle out all oil, except for one large cooking spoon. Add onions, celery, bell pepper, and garlic. Continue cooking, until all vegetables are well-caramelized. Add stock; bring to a boil, and reduce heat, to simmer. Cook approximately 15 minutes, for flavors to develop. Add mushrooms, green onions, and parsley. Season, to taste, using salt. Add rice; reduce heat to very low, and cook (covered) for 30 to 45 minutes, stirring every 15 minutes.

GIANT GINGER COOKIES

4 1/2 cups all-purpose flour
4 teaspoons ground ginger
2 teaspoons baking soda
1 1/2 teaspoons ground cinnamon
1 teaspoon cloves
1/4 teaspoon salt

1 1/2 cups shortening (not butter or margarine, in order to be chewy)
2 cups granulated sugar
2 eggs
1/2 cups molasses
3/4 cup coarse sugar, or granulated sugar

In a medium mixing bowl, stir together the flour, ginger, soda, cinnamon, cloves, and salt. Set aside.

In a large mixing bowl, beat shortening, until softened. Gradually, add the 2 cups granulated sugar; beat, until fluffy. Add eggs and molasses; beat well. Add half of flour mixture; beat, until combined. Stir remaining flour in with a wooden spoon. Using a 1/4-cup ice cream scoop, shape dough into 2-inch balls. Roll in the coarse or granulated sugar. Place on an ungreased cookie sheet about 2 1/2 inches apart.

Bake in a 350-degree oven for 12 to 14 minutes, or until cookies are light brown and puffed. *(Do not overbake, or cookies will not be chewy).* Let stand for 2 minutes before transferring to a wire rack. Cool. Makes 25 four-inch cookies.

David, Melody, and Duke—
Christmas, 1998.

My mother, is special because
"She is the most caring, giving person I've ever known. She is always there when needed by anyone and always puts others first." — *Melody*

If I were not playing football, I'd be a
"Professional fisherman." — *David*

34

Tim & Kendra
LESTER

FULLBACK • 5' 9" • 230

NFL EXPERIENCE
8th year, Los Angeles Raiders
(3), Pittsburgh Steelers (4),
Dallas Cowboys

BIRTHDAY
6-15-68 — *Tim*

COLLEGE
Eastern Kentucky — *Tim*

KIDS
Brandi and Breanna (5)

My friends call me (nickname)
"T-Les." — *Tim*

Tim Lester was known as the "Bus Driver" when he was
the lead blocker for Jerome "The Bus" Bettis in Pittsburgh.

Chef Grady Spears's
SHAKER-BOTTLE PEPPER SAUCE

$^{1}/_{2}$ cup pequin chiles, or other fresh peppers $^{1}/_{2}$ cup white vinegar

Clean a previously used pepper shaker bottle with boiling water. (For larger peppers, such as serranos or habaneros, double the ingredients, and use a pancake syrup dispenser.) Pack the bottle with chiles. Heat the vinegar in a small saucepan, over low heat, until it steams slightly. Pour the vinegar over the chiles to the top of the jar. Allow the mixture to sit for a day before using.

You can use the vinegar as a pepper sauce, or open the bottle to take out a few chiles. The bottle can be refilled with vinegar about 3 times.

It keeps refrigerated for 6 months or more.

SPECIAL EDITION
with Jerry Jones
Saturday 6:30pm

COWBOYS PREGAME SHOW
with Babe Laufenberg
Sunday 10:00am

THE CHAN GAILEY SHOW
Sunday 10:30am

OFFICIAL COWBOYS STATION

11. KTVT CBS

the SCORE
with Babe Laufenberg
Sunday 10:20pm

Leon LETT

ALL-PRO DEFENSIVE END • 6' 6" • 290

NFL EXPERIENCE
6th year, Dallas Cowboys

BIRTHDAY
10-12-68

COLLEGE
Emporia State

KIDS
Shanavia (12)

My hero/heroes are
"Ed 'Too Tall' Jones."

My favorite books/authors are
"Alex Haley."

Favorite food/meal
"Italian, especially lasagna."

My friends call me (nickname)
"Big Cat."

Leon Lett—#78.

Chef Grady Spearss

ICEBERG QUARTERS WITH BUTTERMILK DRESSING

1 head iceberg lettuce
2 cups Buttermilk Dressing (recipe follows)

cracked pepper, to taste

Cut the head of lettuce lengthwise into four quarters. Put each quarter on a salad plate. Pour $^1/_2$ cup of dressing over each quarter and sprinkle with pepper.

BUTTERMILK DRESSING

$^1/_3$ cup minced red onion
2 scallions, thinly-sliced
$^1/_2$ teaspoon roasted garlic, or minced garlic
$^1/_2$ teaspoon dried thyme leaves
1 cup sour cream

$^3/_4$ cup buttermilk
$^1/_2$ cup mayonnaise
kosher salt, to taste
freshly-ground pepper, to taste

Combine all of the ingredients in a bowl; blend with a whisk. The dressing is better if it is allowed to sit in the refrigerator for several hours, to blend flavors, before serving. Store it in the refrigerator in an airtight container; it will keep for about a week.

Mike & Deanna
LUCKY

TIGHT END • 6' 6" • 273

NFL EXPERIENCE
Rookie

BIRTHDAY
11-23-75 — Mike
8-8-77 — Deanna

COLLEGE
Arizona — Mike
Arizona — Deanna

DEANNA'S OCCUPATION
Student - finishing molecular biology degree

KIDS
A baby girl, Madison Romay (due in January, 2000)

Deanna and Mike Lucky.

If you could put your own message on a billboard for all to see, what would it be?
"Never give up." — *Mike*
"Smile—nothing is as bad as it seems." — *Deanna*

All children should be taught to
"Respect authority." — *Mike*
"Respect people of all ages." — *Deanna*

This makes me smile
"My wife." — *Mike*
"My husband." — *Deanna*

If you were stranded on a desert island, three things you would take with you
"My wife, TV, and my bed." — *Mike*
"My scrapbooking supplies, my husband, and all my pictures." — *Deanna*

If you could leave one thing behind for the world to learn from life, it would be
"Don't take anything too seriously." — *Mike*
"Listen to your elders' advice." — *Deanna*

Our plans for the future are
"To raise our baby and give her all our love and values for life that will make her a respectable and lovable person." — *Mike & Deanna*

My hero/heroes are
"My parents." — *Mike*
"My aunt and grandmother." — *Deanna*

My favorite books/authors are
"*The Old Man and the Sea.*" — *Mike*
"Ernest Hemingway—anything." — *Deanna*

First meal my spouse ever prepared for me
"Teriyaki chicken stir-fry over rice." — *Mike*
"Still waiting. . ." — *Deanna*

Favorite food/meal
"Chicken fajitas." — *Mike*
"Santa Fe chicken salad." — *Deanna*

I wish I could sing like
"LeeAnn Rimes." — *Deanna*

My friends call me (nickname)
"Luck Dog." — *Mike*
"Nana." — *Deanna*

MACARONI SALAD

¹/₂ box elbow macaroni	milk
¹/₄ cup celery	mayonnaise
¹/₄ cup green onions	salt and pepper, to taste
¹/₄ cup green pepper	
¹/₄ cup cucumber	OPTIONAL:
a few radishes	¹/₂ can tuna
¹/₂ small can pineapple, crushed	¹/₂ cup shrimp
1 hard-boiled egg	¹/₄ cup tomato

Boil macaroni, until cooked.
Mix all ingredients together; coat with mayonnaise, a little milk, and salt and pepper, to taste.

CHINESE COOKIES

1 6-ounce package chocolate chips	1 cup cocktail peanuts
1 6-ounce package butterscotch chips	1 cup chow mein noodles (canned variety)

Melt together chocolate and butterscotch chips, over low heat, or in double broiler. Add peanuts and noodles; mix well. Drop on wax paper in large tablespoons, to cool and harden.

My ideal vacation

"Cruise to anywhere." — *Mike*

"Cruise to the Greek Islands." — *Deanna*

Hobbies/Other Interests

"Magic tricks, video games, basketball, and watching movies." — *Mike*

"Dancing, arts and crafts, and gymnastics." — *Deanna*

When others describe you, what character qualities do they use?

"Quiet, at first; then, a jokester, and very caring—once you get to know him." — *Mike*

"Friendly, caring, and always looking out for others." — *Deanna*

My wife, is special because

"She treats me like a king, and she makes me a better man." — *Mike*

My husband, is special because

"He is the greatest man in the world, because he puts me before anything and keeps everything exciting." — *Deanna*

I collect

"Stickers." — *Deanna*

If I were not playing football, I'd be a

"Physical Education teacher and a high school football coach." — *Mike*

Deanna and Mike in Maui, Hawaii, after the Hula Bowl (January, 1999).

23 Kevin MATHIS

DEFENSIVE BACK • 5' 9" • 181

NFL EXPERIENCE
3rd year, Dallas Cowboys

BIRTHDAY
4-29-74

COLLEGE
Texas A&M-Commerce

If you could put your own message on a billboard for all to see, what would it be?
"Life on earth is precious and limited, so treasure yours!!"

All children should be taught to
"Value the importance of family, and education is essential."

This makes me smile
"Spending time with family, and seeing others benefit from something I have done."

If you were stranded on a desert island, three things you would take with you
"Bible, flashlight, and blanket."

If you could leave one thing behind for the world to learn from life, it would be
"I would rather try something and fail, then fail by not trying at all!!"

My friends call me (nickname)
"Lil' Fella."

My ideal vacation
"A cruise to the Caribbean Islands for two weeks."

Hobbies/Other Interests
"Playing video games on Sega or PlayStation, and fishing."

I collect
"Video games and CDs."

In 1998, Kevin Mathis established himself as one of the more productive kickoff return men in the NFL.

Chef Grady Spears's

SMOKED TOMATO GUACAMOLE

4 ripe avocados
1 cup minced red onion
1 cup diced Smoked Tomato (recipe follows),
   or 1 cup diced tomato

4 teaspoons freshly-squeezed lemon juice
1 bunch cilantro, stemmed and chopped
kosher salt, to taste

Cut an avocado in half. With a sharp knife, hit the pit so the blade sticks in the seed. Twist the knife slightly; remove and discard the pit. Cut the avocado into small cubes. Scoop out the flesh into a bowl. Repeat with the remaining avocados.

Add the onions and tomatoes to the avocados. Season with salt and lemon juice; add the cilantro. Mix the guacamole, until everything is just incorporated. Serve at once, or hold with plastic wrap on the surface (in a tightly-covered container) for a short time.

Yield: 4 servings.

SMOKED TOMATOES

We use smoked tomatoes in our guacamole, but smoked tomatoes are also the secret of truly great salsas.

Place tomatoes in a stove-top smoker for 7 minutes, or on an outdoor smoker for ¹/₂ hour. Smoking times will vary with the season. Roma tomatoes tend to take longer. Tender summer tomatoes will not take long at all. The result you are looking for is a flavorful, firm tomato, not a cooked tomato.

When others describe you, what character qualities do they use?

"Patience, generosity, and perseverance."

My mother, is special because

"She encourages me to stay confident in all my endeavors and to believe in my ability to succeed in all things."

If I were not playing football, I'd be a

"Middle or high school health teacher and football coach."

I am thankful my parents/grandparents taught me

"My parents taught me to be independent and to trust in God."

83 *Wane* McGARITY

NFL EXPERIENCE
Rookie

BIRTHDAY
9-30-76

COLLEGE
Texas

KIDS
Dominique (4)

Wane holds the Texas Longhorn record for the longest reception (97 yards).

If you could put your own message on a billboard for all to see, what would it be?
"If you believe it, you can achieve it."

All children should be taught to
"Respect their parents."

This makes me smile
"When I see kids having a great time, or visiting elementary schools and children's hospitals."

If you were stranded on a desert island, three things you would take with you
"TV and a VCR."

If you could leave one thing behind for the world to learn from life, it would be
"Never to give up on your dreams."

My plans for the future are
"Have a successful NFL career, finish school, and start a family."

My hero/heroes are
"My mother."

Favorite food/meal
"Enchiladas that my grandma makes."

I wish I could sing like
"Brian McKnight."

My friends call me (nickname)
"Mug."

My ideal vacation
"Nice cruise."

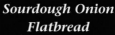

Chef Grady Spear's

SOURDOUGH ONION FLATBREAD

8 cups bread flour
4 teaspoons kosher salt, plus 4 teaspoons, for
sprinkling
6 tablespoons dry yeast
9 cloves garlic, minced
1¼ cups minced scallions (about 1 bunch)

¾ cup minced red onion (about ½ onion)
1 cup Sourdough Starter (page 194)
3 tablespoons olive oil, plus 4 tablespoons,
to brush on dough
2 to 3 cups warm water

Use at least a 5-quart mixing bowl and a mixer with a paddle and dough hook for this recipe. Place all of the ingredients in the mixing bowl, except the water, in the order given. Blend all of the ingredients, using the paddle attachment, with the mixer (at medium-low speed). Begin slowly adding the water, letting it absorb before adding more. As the water is absorbed and the dough comes together, stop the machine and change to the dough hook. Check the dough at this time. It needs to be soft, not dry and crumbly or wet and sticky. Continue adding water, if necessary. The amount of water will vary, depending on the flour and the weather. When the appropriate consistency is reached, turn the mixer speed to low; mix the dough for approximately 15 minutes, or until the dough forms a ball around the top of the hook. The dough should be smooth and very tight.

Lightly oil a large bowl. Pull the dough from the hook. Place it on a smooth, lightly-floured surface, knead it 5 times, and set it in the oiled bowl. Turn the dough once, to oil all sides. Cover the dough loosely with plastic wrap; set it aside in a warm, draft-free area, to proof. The dough should double in bulk in 30 to 45 minutes.

After the dough has risen, punch it down; turn it out onto a lightly-floured smooth surface. Knead the dough several times, rotating it as you go. Portion the dough into 6-ounce balls (for 11 balls total, if you don't have a scale). Let the dough rest for a few minutes. Meanwhile, lightly oil 2 sheet pans (or use parchment paper). Take each dough ball and flatten it to 5 inches across; set it on the prepared pan. Brush the tops with the additional olive oil; sprinkle with salt. Set the dough aside again in a warm place, to let rise until doubled in bulk and about 1½-inches thick. This should take anywhere from 20 to 40 minutes.

During this time, preheat the oven to 375 degrees. Place the bread in the oven; bake for 15 minutes, or until the tops are golden brown.

Yield: 11 flatbreads.

McGarity has come back
from two major knee
operations during college.

NFL EXPERIENCE
6th year, New York Jets (2),
Miami Dolphins (2), Dallas
Cowboys (2)

BIRTHDAY
8-5-70

COLLEGE
Elizabeth City State

KIDS
Everett, Jr. (5), Eric (4),
BriAllen (1)

Despite starting just six games, while battling knee injuries in 1998, the Cowboys learned just how big an impact McIver could have on the offensive line.

All children should be taught to
"Be respectful."

My plans for the future are
"To eat more."

My friends call me (nickname)
"Big Mack."

Hobbies/Other Interests
"Playing football for the NFL."

I collect
"All God's children (Mrs. Martha)."

My mother, is special because
"She can cook."

The Cowboys only allowed six sacks in six games, during the 1998 season, with Everett in the lineup.

Chef Grady Spears's
TORTILLA SOUP

1 whole chicken (about 3 pounds)
6 chicken wings
6 chicken legs or thighs
6 cloves garlic
4 shallots
1 tablespoon whole black peppercorns
1 carrot
3 to 4 quarts water
kosher salt, to taste
freshly-ground pepper, to taste

2 avocados, peeled, seeded, and sliced
    lengthwise into eighths
2 jalapeño peppers, stemmed, seeded, and
    minced
$\frac{1}{4}$ cup oil
6 fresh corn tortillas, cut into thin strips
2 cups (about 8 ounces) grated
    Monterey Jack cheese
1 lime, cut into sixths
$\frac{1}{2}$ bunch cilantro, stemmed, for garnish

In a large, heavy, deep pan, place the washed chicken and chicken pieces. Add the garlic, shallots, peppercorns, carrot, and water. The water should barely cover the chicken. Adjust the amount of water, if necessary.

Place the pan over medium-high heat; bring to a boil. As the water begins to heat, skim any foam that rises to the surface, and discard.

When the water begins to boil, turn the heat down to a constant simmer. Continue skimming, as necessary. Place the cover of the pan slightly ajar; continue cooking for $1\frac{1}{2}$ hours. Turn the heat off; let the chicken sit in the broth for $\frac{1}{2}$ hour, to cool. When the chicken is cool enough to handle, pull the meat off of the bones, discarding the skin and bones. There should be about 3 cups of meat. Set the meat aside (in a covered container that can be heated at serving time). Strain the broth; return it to a clean saucepan. Skim off any fat that has accumulated on the surface. There should be about 2 quarts of broth. Season with salt and pepper.

At serving time, reheat the chicken. Heat the broth to boiling, and keep hot. Prepare all of the vegetables. If you have sensitive skin, wear gloves when handling the hot peppers. In a large skillet, heat the oil.

When the oil is hot, add the tortilla strips; sauté until crisp, turning them once or twice. Remove the strips; drain them on paper towels. Repeat, if necessary. Have all of the soup ingredients ready to assemble at serving time, as you will "build" each soup bowl individually. In the bottom of the bowl, place $\frac{3}{4}$ cup chicken meat. Arrange avocado slices around the meat. Sprinkle with $\frac{1}{2}$ cup cheese, diced jalapeño, and top with a wedge of lime. Ladle hot broth over all. Place a handful of crispy tortilla strips in the center. Top with a garnish of cilantro leaves. Serve at once.

Yield: 4 servings.

82

James & Mikki
McKNIGHT

WIDE RECEIVER • 6' 1" • 198

NFL EXPERIENCE
6th year, Seattle Seahawks (5),
Dallas Cowboys (1)

BIRTHDAY
6-17-72 — *James*
7-8-75 — *Mikki*

COLLEGE
Liberty — *James*

KIDS
David Sexton (7)

PETS
Patience - Cocker Spaniel

James and Mikki—our wedding day (June 20, 1998).

If you could put your own message on a billboard for all to see, what would it be?

"To love others is to love yourself." — *James*

"If you can't count on anyone else in the world, the one thing you can take to the bank, is that God is God, and He's always there." — *Mikki*

All children should be taught to

"Obey their parents and respect others." — *James*

"Love God, obey His word, stand in faith, and let Him direct your path." — *Mikki*

My favorite books/authors are

"Bible" — *James*

"Terry McMillan—all her books; *Blessings,* by Sheneska Jackson." — *Mikki*

This makes me smile

"My wife, my son, and worship service at my church." — *James*

"How excited Patience gets when James comes home from work, or the car, or even from the other room!" — *Mikki*

If you were stranded on a desert island, three things you would take with you

"My Bible, my wife, and a tent." — *James*

"My Bible, Red Vines, oh . . . and my husband!" — *Mikki*

If you could leave one thing behind for the world to learn from life, it would be

"Don't live for today, store wealth for your children's children." — *James*

"Please learn to love one another—in heaven we'll be treated all the same." — *Mikki*

David, James, and Alberta,
(James' mom) eating after a game.

40th Anniversary

Chef Grady Spears's
CAJETA POUND CAKE

1½ cups unsalted butter, softened
3 cups sugar
8 eggs
4 cups sifted flour

2 teaspoons baking powder
1 teaspoon kosher salt
2 cups Cajeta Sauce (page 56)

Preheat the oven to 350 degrees. Grease the inside of a Bundt pan. Dust lightly with flour, shake out excess, and set aside. Cream the butter and sugar in a mixer, fitted with a paddle attachment, until the mixture is light in color and texture. Add the eggs, one at a time, blending well after each addition. Stop and scrape the bowl with a spatula, as needed. Beat the mixture, until it is light in color (about 3 minutes). Sift the flour, baking powder, and salt together; then, add to the creamed mixture, blending (at low speed). Increase the speed; beat the mixture for 2 minutes. Fold in the Cajeta Sauce, with the mixer running at the lowest speed.

Pour batter into the prepared pan. Bake the cake for 1 hour and 15 minutes. Begin to test cake after 1 hour, with a toothpick. An inserted toothpick will come out clean when the cake is done. Remove the cake from the oven; let it cool. Turn the cake out onto a serving plate. The cake may be chilled in the refrigerator.

Yield: 1 Bundt cake, about 12 servings.

Our plans for the future are
"Have children, and to devote our time showing others God's love and mercy by the way we live our lives." — *James & Mikki*

My hero/heroes are
"My mother and Jesus, for the lives they live." — *James*
"God Almighty—He made the ultimate sacrifice, and I'll always honor Him." — *Mikki*

First meal my spouse ever prepared for me
"Lasagna, with salad and garlic French bread, and chicken wings." — *James*
"Beef ribs, macaroni & cheese, cajun rice, and cornbread." — *Mikki*

Favorite food/meal
"Spaghetti and lasagna." — *James*
"Lasagna." — *Mikki*

I wish I could sing like
"Kenny Lattimore." — *James*
"Stephanie Mills." — *Mikki*

My friends call me (nickname)
"J-Roc." — *James*
"Auntie Mikki." — *Mikki*

I collect
"Baseball cards." — *James*
"African-American art; figurines." — *Mikki*

My ideal vacation
"Anywhere alone with my wife and no phones." — *James*
"Where desserts are the main course, everything is free, and I can stay as long as I want." — *Mikki*

Hobbies/Other Interests
"Basketball, track, and art." — *James*
"Working out, reading, drawing, and cooking." — *Mikki*

When others describe you, what character qualities do they use?
"Spirited, joy to be around, always making them laugh, loving, and caring." — *James*
"Respectable, sisterly, honest, loveable, and a bag of giggles." — *Mikki*

My mother, is special because
"She is my mother, my father, and my friend." — *James*

80

Ernie
MILLS

NFL EXPERIENCE
9th year, Pittsburgh Steelers
(6), Carolina Panthers (1),
Dallas Cowboys (2)

BIRTHDAY
10-28-68

COLLEGE
Florida

KIDS
Erin (newborn)

Mills was a teammate of Emmitt Smith at the University of Florida.

If you could put your own message on a billboard for all to see, what would it be?
"Thank you, Jesus, for your blessings today."

All children should be taught to
"Respect their parents and elders."

This makes me smile
"Being around my family and watching the growth of the kids in my family."

If you could leave one thing behind for the world to learn from life, it would be
"Forgiveness."

My/Our plans for the future are
"To always be positive, and encouraging our youth to be the best as they can be."

My hero/heroes are
"Dr. Martin Luther King, Jr."

My favorite books/authors are
"*Their Eyes Were Watching God,* by Zora Neale Hurston. "

Favorite food/meal
"Neckbones, on occasion; some form of chicken everyday."

Erin Mills.

Chef Grady Spears's

BACON-WRAPPED SHRIMP WITH ONION MARMALADE

12 shrimp (about 1 pound), peeled, with tails left on
12 thin slices smoked bacon

1½ cups Onion Marmalade (page 198)

Prepare a grill. The temperature should be medium-high. Clean and de-vein the shrimp. Wrap bacon tightly around each shrimp. Preheat the oven to 500 degrees. Place the shrimp on the grill; cook them for 5 minutes. Turn them over; cook an additional 5 minutes. The bacon should be browned and crisp. Make sure the shrimp do not catch on fire from the bacon drippings igniting. Remove the shrimp to a sheet pan; place them in the preheated oven, to finish cooking, for 4 minutes, or until the bacon is cooked. Serve two shrimp with ¼ cup of marmalade per person as an appetizer.

Yield: 6 servings.

My friends call me (nickname)

"Mills, Ned, Fernando, Sleezy (Slow and Easy)."

My ideal vacation

"The islands with no phones, emergencies, or worries."

Hobbies/Other Interests

"Driving long distance, bowling, and golf."

When others describe you, what character qualities do they use?

"Quiet, calm, relaxed, and look like I'm not worried about anything."

My mother, is special because

" She's positive, supportive, and a strong single mother. "

If I were not playing football, I'd be a

"Athletic director of a high school or small college."

I am thankful my parents/grandparents taught me

"Faith, strength, and courage."

Ernie graduated from Florida with a degree in sports administration/exercise and sports science.

Singor MOBLEY

DEFENSIVE BACK • 5' 11" • 195

NFL EXPERIENCE
3rd year, Dallas Cowboys

BIRTHDAY
10-12-72

COLLEGE
Washington State

PETS
Denali - Mastiff

All children should be taught to
"Obey their parents."

This makes me smile
"Being around my friends."

If you were stranded on a desert island, three things you would take with you
"1—some company; 2—games; and 3—books."

My plans for the future are
"To own a business."

Favorite food/meal
"Chicken and rice."

My friends call me (nickname)
"Sing."

My ideal vacation
"Milan, Italy."

Hobbies/Other Interests
"Snowboarding."

If I were not playing football, I'd be a
"Firefighter."

I am thankful my parents/grandparents taught me
"What's right and what's wrong."

Singor Mobley finished 1998 with 10 special teams tackles.

Chef Grady Spears's YALLER BREAD WITH PINTOS

1½ cups buttermilk
3 eggs, lightly-beaten
3 tablespoons sugar
1 teaspoon baking soda
½ cup Ranch Beans (page 104)

½ cup fresh corn kernels
1 cup flour
1½ cups fine yellow cornmeal
½ cup melted butter

Preheat the oven to 375 degrees. Combine the buttermilk, eggs, sugar, and soda; mix well. Add the beans and corn. Sift together the flour and cornmeal. Slowly add the flour mixture to the liquids, whisking until well-incorporated. Whisk in the melted butter. Pour the batter into a greased 8 by 8-inch pan or cast-iron skillet; bake for 40 minutes, or until a toothpick comes out clean.
Yield: 8 large squares.

Bob & Mary Breunig

Supporting the children at

Happy Hill Farm Academy / Home
since 1978

NFL EXPERIENCE
Rookie

BIRTHDAY
8-4-75

COLLEGE
Air Force Academy

Three happy Morgans in cabin in Colorado Springs (June, 1999). Beau with his brother, Blane, and sister, Brooke.

If you could put your own message on a billboard for all to see, what would it be?
"Soli Deo Gloria."

All children should be taught to
"Pray, be thankful, and act selflessly."

This makes me smile
"Bob Wylie."

If you were stranded on a desert island, three things you would take with you
"A hammock, a snorkel, and a good book."

If you could leave one thing behind for the world to learn from life, it would be
"Fear God and keep His commandments."

My plans for the future are
"Live one day at a time under the grace of God."

My hero/heroes are
"Father, Paul, Joe Montana, Dee Dowis, Mike Singletary, and Abraham Lincoln."

My favorite books/authors are
"Authors: Apostle Paul, Albert Camus, and Plato. Books: *Flow—The Psychology of Optimal Experience, Mere Christianity, Crime and Punishment, Romans,* and *Proverbs.*"

Favorite food/meal
"Any that are free and already prepared."

I wish I could sing like
"Enrico Palatzo."

My friends call me (nickname)
"Bobo or Beau."

Blane—with Michael, and Beau—with Matt, in Colorado Springs in 1998.

CHICKEN ENCHILADAS

1 whole chicken, or 3 good-size chicken breasts
2 packages of 18-count flour tortillas
1 8-ounce container sour cream, or light sour cream
1 package Lawry's or McCormick's enchilada sauce mix

1 medium-size can chopped green chilies
1 can cream of mushroom soup
3 small (8-ounce) cans tomato sauce
Mexican cheese, grated
$1/2$ cup oil

Cook chicken, take off bone, and set aside. Heat enchilada sauce in a sauce pan; add tomato sauce, sour cream, mushroom soup, and green chilies, and set aside.

Heat oil in skillet. When hot, place each tortilla in the oil (for only a second) and remove—you want them soft, but not hard. Drain tortillas on paper towels. Place enchilada sauce mix inside each tortilla, add chicken; and roll, to close. Place in a baking dish. Cover with grated cheese. Bake at 350 degrees for 20-30 minutes. Cover dish with foil.

Makes approximately 36 enchiladas. If you don't want this many, you may freeze leftover sauce mix and use later.

This is Beau's favorite dish—submitted by his mom, Mary Morgan.

Beau with Dad—Barry, and sister—
Brooke, in Hawaii
(Christmas, 1998).

My ideal vacation
"Tropical, long, and quiet."

Hobbies/Other Interests
"Reading, spending time with friends and family, and sports."

I collect
"Books."

When others describe you, what character qualities do they use?
"I don't know—you would have to ask them."

My mother, is special because
"She rarely puts her own desires ahead of anyone else's, and she loves me unconditionally."

If I were not playing football, I'd be a
"Coach."

I am thankful my parents/grandparents taught me
"Discipline, ethics, and absolute truth."

94

Michael & Brandy MYERS

DEFENSIVE TACKLE • 6' 2" • 288

NFL EXPERIENCE
2nd year, Dallas Cowboys

BIRTHDAY
1-20-76 — *Michael*
7-25-73 — *Brandy*

COLLEGE
Alabama — *Michael*
Stillman College — *Brandy*

BRANDY'S OCCUPATION
Leasing Agent

Brandy and Michael during their honeymoon on a Bahamas cruise (1999).

All children should be taught to
"Be respectful." — *Michael*
"Strive to accomplish their endeavors." — *Brandy*

This makes me smile
"When I am blessed to wake up to a new day." — *Michael*
"When Michael is being successful with his career." — *Brandy*

If you could leave one thing behind for the world to learn from life, it would be
"To overcome adversity." — *Michael*
"To respect one another." — *Brandy*

Our plans for the future are
"To have a family." — *Michael & Brandy*

My hero/heroes are
"My father, Ernest Lewis, Sr." — *Michael*

Favorite food/meal
"Fried chicken." — *Michael*
"Spaghetti." — *Brandy*

Hobbies/Other Interests
"Swimming and basketball." — *Michael*
"Volleyball and basketball." — *Brandy*

I collect
"CDs." — *Michael*
"Elephants." — *Brandy*

I am thankful my parents/grandparents taught me
"To have patience." — *Michael*
"The importance of an education." — *Brandy*

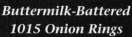

Chef Grady Spears's

BUTTERMILK-BATTERED 1015 ONION RINGS

2 large 1015 onions
1½ cups Flour Spice (page 145)
4 eggs
1 cup buttermilk
1 cup Shiner Bock beer, or any good bock beer

1 teaspoon salt
5 cups peanut oil
kosher salt, to taste
freshly-ground pepper, to taste

Cut the two ends off of the onions; discard. Slice the onions, to produce rings about 1½-inches thick. Remove the very center of the onion; discard. Separate the rings; set aside. Put the flour spice in a bowl, or on a plate; set it aside. Prepare the batter by whisking together the eggs, buttermilk, beer, and salt. Heat the oil in a heavy, deep saucepan, or deep-fat fryer, to a temperature of 350 degrees, or until a drop of batter sizzles when dropped in it. When the correct temperature is reached, begin the breading process with the onion rings. Dip each ring into the batter, dredge it in the Flour Spice, place it back into the batter, and again into the Flour Spice. The final dredging should evenly coat the batter, so the rings are dry on the outside. Slide the prepared rings into the hot oil. Fry the rings for 4 to 6 minutes, maintaining an even temperature, until they are golden brown. Remove the rings with a skimmer or slotted spoon, as they become golden brown, to drain on a tray—lined with paper towels. When all of the onion rings are cooked, stack them on a serving platter.

During the Washington game, on 12-27-98, Myers was teamed with Greg Ellis to become the first pair of rookie defensive linemen to start at the same time in club history.

39 *Ryan* NEUFELD

FULLBACK • 6'4" • 240

NFL EXPERIENCE
Rookie

BIRTHDAY
11-22-75

COLLEGE
UCLA

Ryan with fiancée—Dawn, and
his parents—Sandra and Roger.

If you could put your own message on a billboard for all to see, what would it be?
"Never give up!"

All children should be taught to
"Respect authority (parents, teachers, etc.)."

This makes me smile
"My fiancée, family, and friends."

If you could leave one thing behind for the world to learn from life, it would be
"That life is full of obstacles and adversity, and it's how we deal with that adversity that determines our success."

My plans for the future are
"Get married to my fiancée, and buy a house."

My hero is
"My father."

Favorite food/meal
"Pizza."

I wish I could sing like
"I just wish I could sing."

My friends call me (nickname)
"Neu."

My ideal vacation
"Being in the woods next to a lake in a log cabin, sleeping in, and going fishing."

Hobbies/Other Interests
"Fishing."

My mother and father, are special because
"They have always supported me in everything I've done—never missed a game I've played since I was a kid—and they have worked hard to give me everything I needed."

If I were not playing football, I'd be a
"Pursuing a career as a firefighter."

WALDORF ASTORIA CAKE

CAKE:
1½ cups sugar
½ cup vegetable shortening
2 cups cake flour
2 tablespoons cocoa
1 teaspoon salt
1 ounce water

FROSTING:
1 cup milk
¼ cup flour
⅛ teaspoon salt

1 ounce red food coloring
1 cup buttermilk
2 eggs
1 teaspoon vanilla
1 tablespoon vinegar
1 teaspoon baking soda

1 cup sugar
1 cup butter
1 teaspoon vanilla

CAKE: Combine sugar, shortening, flour, cocoa, salt, pre-mixed water and food coloring, and ²⁄₃ cup of buttermilk in mixing bowl. Beat, until well-blended. Add eggs, remainder of buttermilk, and vanilla; beat for one minute. Mix vinegar and baking soda; stir into batter by hand. *Do not beat.* Pour into two 9-inch greased pans. Bake 30 minutes in a preheated 350-degree oven.

FROSTING: Combine flour and salt; add milk gradually. Cook, while stirring, until thick. Cool; beat with mixer. Add sugar, butter, and vanilla. Beat, until fluffy. Spread on cake, and garnish with nuts or coconut.

I am thankful my parents/grandparents taught me
"Never to quit and to always put forth my best effort."

Ryan with sisters—Stephanie and Veronica, and Veronica's husband—Billy.

64

Robert & Shywana
NEWKIRK

DEFENSIVE LINEMAN • 6' 3" • 290

NFL EXPERIENCE
Rookie

BIRTHDAY
3-6-77 — *Robert*
1-29-77 — *Shywana*

COLLEGE
Michigan State — *Robert*
Michigan State — *Shywana*

SHYWANA'S OCCUPATION
Educator/Family & Child
Specialist

KIDS
Raégine Shynelle Rose

The Newkirk Family.

If you could put your own message on a billboard for all to see, what would it be?
"All men were created equal, but . . . ." — *Robert*
"Love thy neighbor." — *Shywana*

All children should be taught to
"Respect their elders, and be disciplined by both parents." — *Robert*
"Respect their elders." — *Shywana*

This makes me smile
"My uncle Frank 'Money' Huggins." — *Robert*
"Watching my daughter learn different things in life." — *Shywana*

If you were stranded on a desert island, three things you would take with you
"A spear, water, and a camel." — *Robert*
"Robert, Raégine, and TV." — *Shywana*

If you could leave one thing behind for the world to learn from life, it would be
"Take full advantage of opportunities in life." — *Robert*
"You can reach your goal with hard work." — *Shywana*

Our plans for the future are
"Be the best parents, and a friend to our siblings." — *Robert & Shywana*

My hero/heroes are
"Jesus Christ, and Daniel Calloway." — *Robert*
"My mother, Darlene Buchanan." — *Shywana*

My favorite books/authors are
"*Seven Habits of Highly-Effective People.*" — *Robert*

First meal my spouse ever prepared for me
"Lasagna with extra cheese— prepared at 1 A.M." — *Robert*
"Juicy sirloin steak with white rice." — *Shywana*

Favorite food/meal
"Lasagna, with extra cheese, and French bread." — *Robert*
"Lasagna." — *Shywana*

MIKKI'S MUST-BE-HEAVEN CHOCOLATE CHIP COOKIES

1 cup Butter-Flavored Crisco, or butter
1 cup sugar
1 cup brown sugar
2 eggs
1 teaspoon vanilla
2 cups flour
2½ cups oatmeal, blended,
    until it turns to powder

½ teaspoon salt
1½ teaspoons baking powder
1 teaspoon baking soda
1 12-ounce bag of chocolate chips
1½ cups of nuts, chopped, your choice

Preheat oven to 350 degrees.
Cream together Crisco, sugar, and brown sugar. Add eggs and vanilla; set aside.
In a separate bowl, combine flour, oatmeal, salt, baking powder, and baking soda.
Mix all ingredients together.
Place tablespoon-size cookies (approximately 2 inches) apart on an ungreased cookie sheet.
Bake for 6 to 9 minutes. Makes approximately 50 cookies.

I wish I could sing like

"Billy Dee Williams." — *Robert*

"Mary J. Blige." — *Shywana*

My friends call me (nickname)

"Bobby New, D.U., M.L., and C.B." — *Robert*

"Shay-Shay." — *Shywana*

My ideal vacation

"US Virgin Islands, St. John, St. Thomas, and St. Croix—sailing from island to island with a good supply of Heinekens." — *Robert*

"Jamaica." — *Shywana*

Hobbies/Other Interests

"Studying and maintaining plant material; like to work on automobiles—older cars." — *Robert*

"Dinner—going out, movies, and talking with others." — *Shywana*

Shywana and Robert Newkirk.

I collect

"Everything . . . it seems like it—ask my wife." — *Robert*

"Teddy bears and ceramic figures." — *Shywana*

When others describe you, what character qualities do they use?

"For some reason, people usually describe me as a smooth talker or, as some would say, easy to get along with others." — *Robert*

"As a very humorous, warm-hearted person." — *Shywana*

My mother and grandmother, are special because

"I understand them very well, and I can relate to their lifestyle and social behavior." — *Robert*

My mother and grandmother, are special because

"They care, are willing to listen to me, and care about my feelings." — *Shywana*

59 *Dat* NGUYEN

LINEBACKER • 5' 11" • 231

NFL EXPERIENCE
Rookie

BIRTHDAY
9-25-75

COLLEGE
Texas A&M

Dat won the 1998 Lombardi Trophy and the Chuck Bednarik Award.

If you could put your own message on a billboard for all to see, what would it be?
"Believe in yourself—don't listen to others that are negative about your ambitions."

All children should be taught to
"Socialize with others."

This makes me smile
"When I put a smile on a kid's face."

If you were stranded on a desert island, three things you would take with you
"Water, PlayStation, and TV."

If you could leave one thing behind for the world to learn from life, it would be
"Live everyday to the meaningness."

My/Our plans for the future are
"To have my own business."

My hero/heroes are
"Michael Jordan."

My favorite books/authors are
"*Chicken Soup for the Soul.*"

Favorite food/meal
"Rice and charbroiled chicken."

I wish I could sing like
"Tyrese."

My friends call me (nickname)
"Mop (fat boy in Vietnamese)."

My ideal vacation
"To visit Southeast Asia."

Hobbies/Other Interests
"Video games, golf, and spending time with friends."

I collect
"Old pennies (1960)."

When others describe you, what character qualities do they use?
"Kind, trustworthy, friendly, and sociable."

My mother, is special because
"She helps me see the future, rather than just what was in front of me."

If I were not playing football, I'd be a
"Finishing up my Masters in college."

I am thankful my parents/grandparents taught me
"To treat others the way I would like to be treated."

Chef Grady Spears's

CHICKEN GUMBO

10 tablespoons unsalted butter
⅔ cup flour
2 cups diced red bell pepper
2 cups diced green bell pepper
3 cups diced onion
2 stalks celery, diced
2 15-ounce cans diced tomatoes
5 tablespoons Worcestershire sauce
2 tablespoons Tabasco sauce
2 tablespoons tomato paste

1 bay leaf
2 teaspoons dried thyme leaves
2 teaspoons dried oregano leaves
1 teaspoon ground cayenne pepper
1 teaspoon ground white pepper
6 cups chicken stock
meat from two whole cooked chickens, diced
    or pulled off the bone
kosher salt, to taste
freshly-ground pepper, to taste

Use a large, heavy pan that will hold at least 4 quarts. Melt the butter in the pan, over medium heat. Stir in the flour, and cook, over medium-low heat, for about 20 minutes (or longer). The roux needs to become a rich brown color, without burning. Continual stirring with a wooden spoon is necessary. This step is what gives the gumbo its color and flavor. When the roux is the desired color, add the peppers, onion, and celery, sautéing until the vegetables are wilted (about 10 minutes). Next, add the tomatoes, Worcestershire, Tabasco, tomato paste, bay leaf, thyme, oregano, cayenne, and white pepper. Stir, to blend these ingredients. Whisk in the chicken stock, and cook the gumbo, over medium heat, for 30 minutes. Add the chicken meat; continue cooking for another 30 minutes. Season with salt and pepper. The gumbo should be fairly thick at serving time. Continue cooking, to reduce, if necessary. Serve at once over rice or mashed potatoes.

Dat was also named the National and
Big XII Defensive Player of the Year in 1998.

75 *Brandon* NOBLE

DEFENSIVE TACKLE • 6' 2" • 285

NFL EXPERIENCE
1st year, Dallas Cowboys

BIRTHDAY
4-10-74

COLLEGE
Penn State

Brandon spent this spring with the Barcelona Dragons of NFL Europe.

If you could put your own message on a billboard for all to see, what would it be?
"Slow down and enjoy life."

This makes me smile
"My fiancée, Mary Kate."

My plans for the future are
"Play football as long as possible, get married, and start a family."

My hero/heroes are
"My parents."

My favorite books/authors are
"*The Lord of the Rings,* by Tolkien."

Favorite food/meal
"My mother's Cheese Chicken."

My ideal vacation
"A couple of weeks fishing in Canada."

Hobbies/Other Interests
"Fishing and reading."

When others describe you, what character qualities do they use?
"Laid back, good natured, and hard working."

My fiancée, is special because
"She has put up with me and my attempt to make it in the NFL. "

If I were not playing football, I'd be a
"Policeman, teacher, or coach—I'm not really sure."

Chef Grady Spears's
RANCH BEANS

4 cups dried pinto beans
4 cups minced yellow onions, plus 1 1/2 cups, diced
1/2 cup pure chile powder
1/4 cup kosher salt

1/2 bunch cilantro, stemmed and chopped
4 tablespoons olive oil
2 cups diced red bell pepper
2 cups diced green bell pepper

Wash the beans; sort through them, to remove any foreign particles and broken beans. In a stockpot, cover the beans with cold water by 6 inches; soak them 6 hours, or overnight. Be sure the beans remain covered with water during the soaking process. Drain the beans, and return them to the same pan. Cover them with fresh water by 1 1/2 inches. Add the minced onions, chile powder, salt, and cilantro; stir, to blend. Bring the beans to a boil (over medium heat). Reduce heat, cover, and cook, until the beans are tender (about 2 1/2 hours). From time to time, check and stir the beans. If necessary, add water as needed. Near the end of the cooking time, the liquid should be almost absorbed. Close to serving time, heat the olive oil in a large sauté pan. When the oil is very hot, add the diced onion and peppers; cook them quickly (about 6 minutes) stirring and tossing, until crisp but tender. Stir this mixture into the beans. Serve at once.

I am thankful my parents/grandparents taught me
"To respect other people and to enjoy life."

As a senior at Penn State, in 1996, Noble posted a
team-high 8 sacks and a career-high 72 tackles.

85 *Jeff* OGDEN

WIDE RECEIVER • 6' 0" • 190

NFL EXPERIENCE
2nd year, Dallas Cowboys

BIRTHDAY
2-22-75

COLLEGE
Eastern Washington

PETS
Hallie Girl - Fish

Jeff relaxing in the off-season
in the Spokane countryside.

If you could put your own message on a billboard for all to see, what would it be?
"Life is short . . . pray hard!"

All children should be taught to
"Serve God, honor their parents, and love one another."

This makes me smile
"Seeing my family dressed up in Cowboys gear from head to toe."

If you were stranded on a desert island, three things you would take with you
"Bible, a cook, and Leatherman."

If you could leave one thing behind for the world to learn from life, it would be
"Live, love, and relate today as if there will be no tomorrow."

My plans for the future are
"Coach high school football, and fish and golf in the summer at my cabin in Montana."

My hero/heroes are
"Gideon."

My favorite books/authors are
"Book: *The Edge*; Author: Howard Ferguson."

Favorite food/meal
"Steak on the grill and fruit salad."

I wish I could sing like
"Elvis."

My friends call me (nickname)
"Oggie."

My ideal vacation
"A week on a Turkish golf course."

Hobbies/Other Interests
"Building furniture, and golfing."

My mother, is special because
"She rises above all challenges and has a genuine concern for the welfare of others."

If I were not playing football, I'd be a
"Graduate student."

Jeff Ogden
Chicken Manicotti
Layered Pudding Dessert

Jeff's "Little" Fan Club—nephew, Nathan; nephew, Matthew; and niece, MacKenzie.

CHICKEN MANICOTTI

box of manicotti shells
4 cups cooked chicken breast meat, or 3 packages of Louis Rich Italian Seasoned Chicken Strips

1 jar spaghetti sauce
1 cup Mozzarella cheese, shredded
1 cup Cheddar cheese, shredded

Preheat oven to 350 degrees.

Boil manicotti shells in water, until soft. Mix together ¾ jar of spaghetti sauce with cooked chicken meat, and stuff the manicotti shells. Pour the remaining sauce over the shells. Top with grated cheese; bake for 35-45 minutes.

LAYERED PUDDING DESSERT

2 cubes butter, not margarine
2 cups walnuts, chopped
2 cups flour
1 8-ounce package cream cheese, softened
1 cup powdered sugar

1 large tub of Cool Whip
1 small package instant chocolate pudding
1 small package instant vanilla pudding
3 cups milk

Mix together butter, walnuts, and flour; pat in a 9x13-inch baking dish, and bake at 350 degrees, until golden brown. Set aside, to cool.

Mix cream cheese, powdered sugar, and half the tub of Cool Whip; spread over cooled crust.

Mix puddings and milk together until thick; spread over the top.

Spread remaining Cool Whip on top, and sprinkle with chopped nuts or shredded chocolate bar.

I am thankful my parents/grandparents taught me

"That dreams can come true, and it was up to me to make it happen."

Cowboys vs. the Eagles—December 20, 1998.

77

PAGE

OFFENSIVE LINEMAN • 6' 4" • 304

NFL EXPERIENCE
Rookie

BIRTHDAY
2-27-76

COLLEGE
West Virginia

Solomon Page was an athletic coaching
education major at West Virginia.

Chef Grady Spears's
RED CHILE SAUCE

2 cups Red Chile Paste (see page 51)
1 cup diced tomato
1 teaspoon ground cumin

1 tablespoon honey
kosher salt, to taste
2 tablespoons oil

Place the chile paste, tomato, cumin, and honey in a blender; purée, until smooth. Adjust seasonings with salt. Heat the oil in a skillet over medium-high heat. Pour in the purée; cook it for 3 minutes, until the flavors are well-combined. Use the sauce **immediately** on enchiladas, or store in a glass container in the refrigerator, until ready to use. Keeps for 1 week.

This is a classic red sauce that can be used for any kind of enchiladas.

Yield: about 3 cups.

ADVERTISING

ANNUAL REPORTS

CATALOGS

GENO LORO JR.
PHOTOGRAPHY
817-332-8171

Joe PHIPPS

LINEBACKER • 6'1" • 220

NFL EXPERIENCE
Rookie

BIRTHDAY
11-24-75

COLLEGE
TCU

If you could put your own message on a billboard for all to see, what would it be?
"Play hard."

All children should be taught to
"Respect their parents and other adults."

This makes me smile
"Seeing my mother happy."

If you were stranded on a desert island, three things you would take with you
"TV, lifetime supply of Hawaiian Punch, and a comfortable couch."

My hero/heroes are
"My parents"

If you could leave one thing behind for the world to learn from life, it would be
"Do your best when you can."

My plans for the future are
"To become the best football player I can be."

When others describe you, what character qualities do they use?
"Honest and laid back."

My favorite books/authors are
"Tom Clancy books."

Favorite food/meal
"Fried chicken, collard greens, mac and cheese, mashed potatoes and gravy, and cornbread."

Joe Phipps led the Horned Frogs in tackles each of his last two seasons.

Chef Grady Spears's MANGO VINAIGRETTE

½ cup cider vinegar
2 teaspoons Dijon mustard
½ teaspoon minced garlic
1½ teaspoons honey
1 teaspoon freshly-squeezed lime juice
1 cup peeled, ripe mango pieces, plus
 ¼ cup peeled, finely-diced ripe mango

1½ cups olive oil
½ cup minced cilantro leaves
½ habanero pepper, stemmed, seeded, and
 minced
2 tablespoons thinly-sliced scallions
kosher salt, to taste

Put the vinegar, mustard, garlic, honey, lime juice, and 1 cup ripe mango in a blender. Blend, at medium speed. With the motor running, remove the top, and slowly drizzle in the olive oil. The mixture should be thick and emulsified. Fold the cilantro, habaneros, scallions, and diced mango into the dressing. If the dressing is too thick, thin with water.

Serve at once, or store the dressing; it will keep for up to 4 days.

Yield: 4 cups.

97

Kavika PITTMAN

DEFENSIVE END • 6' 6" • 273

NFL EXPERIENCE
4th year, Dallas Cowboys

BIRTHDAY
2-9-74

COLLEGE
McNeese State

All children should be taught to
"Stay in school, because life is not easy, and they will need an education to survive."

My hero/heroes are
"Michael Jordan."

Favorite food/meal
"Smothered pork chop, mashed potatoes with brown gravy, and green beans."

My ideal vacation
"Columbus, Georgia—because all of my friends are there."

Hobbies/Other Interests
"Video games."

If I were not playing football, I'd be a
"I think that I would be coaching football somewhere."

Kavika Pittman was born in Frankfurt, Germany.

Chef Grady Spears's
SALSA VERDE

1 pound tomatillos (about 13)	1½ teaspoons minced garlic
¼ bunch cilantro, stems removed, leaves chopped	¼ cup red bell pepper, cut into ⅛-inch cubes
3 fresh serrano chiles, stemmed and chopped	2 tablespoons honey
½ cup thinly-sliced scallions (about 5 scallions)	1 teaspoon freshly-squeezed lime juice
	kosher salt, to taste

Husk the tomatillos by removing the parchmentlike covering on the outside. Rinse them; place them in a saucepan. Just cover them with water. Bring the water to a boil, reduce the heat; allow the tomatillos to simmer for 3 to 5 minutes, or until they are just tender, but still green in color. Remove them from heat, drain them, and coarsely chop them in a food processor. Pour the tomatillos into a bowl; add the cilantro, chiles, scallions, garlic, bell pepper, honey, and lime juice. Mix well. Season with salt. Will keep for up to a week in the refrigerator.

Yield: 2 cups.

11

Mike QUINN

NFL EXPERIENCE
3rd year, Pittsburgh Steelers
(1), Dallas Cowboys (2)

BIRTHDAY
4-15-74

COLLEGE
Stephen F. Austin St.

PETS
Smokey - Weimaraner

Mike with his mom and two sisters.

If you could put your own message on a billboard for all to see, what would it be?
"Hey! How's it going?"

All children should be taught to
"Live by the Golden Rule."

This makes me smile
"Genuine politeness."

If you were stranded on a desert island, three things you would take with you
"My dog, Smokey, his football, and the book, *Primitive Shipbuilding for Dummies*."

If you could leave one thing behind for the world to learn from life, it would be
"Trust God."

My plans for the future are
"Get married someday and start a family."

My hero/heroes are
"My mom."

My favorite books/authors are
"The *Left Behind* series, by LaHaye and Jenkins."

Favorite food/meal
"French fries."

I wish I could sing like
"Dave Matthews."

My friends call me (nickname)
"Q."

My ideal vacation
"Tropical cruise."

Hobbies/Other Interests
"Golf, reading, drawing, traveling, movies, and music."

My mother, is special because
"She put up with a lot raising me and my two older sisters, and worked very hard as a single mother to provide for us."

Chef Grady Spears's
PECAN PIE

¹/₂ recipe Piecrust (page 36)	4 cups dark corn syrup
6 eggs	1¹/₂ teaspoons vanilla extract
¹/₂ cup sugar	¹/₂ teaspoon kosher salt
¹/₂ cup flour	2 cups chopped pecans

Preheat the oven to 400 degrees. Lightly butter a 9-inch pie pan. Roll out the piecrust dough to fit the pan. Put the dough into the pan, trim, and flute the edges. Set aside.

In a mixer with a paddle attachment, beat the eggs, until well-combined and light in color (about 5 minutes). Mix the sugar and flour together; gradually add to the eggs, using low speed. Add the corn syrup, vanilla, and salt; blend well, again using low speed. Fold the nuts in by hand, and pour the mixture into the prepared piecrust. Bake at 400 degrees for 10 minutes; then, reduce the heat to 350 degrees, and bake for 1 hour longer. The pie will rise up and form cracks on the top, and the filling will be set, when baking is complete. Add additional time, if the center looks too runny. A knife inserted into the center will come out moist but clean, when the pie is cooked. Remove from the oven, and let cool before serving.

I am thankful my parents/grandparents taught me
"The value of hard work."

Mike came to Dallas with the knowledge of Chan Gailey's offense after serving as the Steelers' third quarterback in 1997.

43

Izell REESE

DEFENSIVE BACK • 6' 2" • 196

NFL EXPERIENCE
2nd year, Dallas Cowboys

BIRTHDAY
5-7-74

COLLEGE
Alabama-Birmingham

All children should be taught to
"Never settle for second best. There's nothing wrong with envisioning goals; just put it in perspective."

My plans for the future are
"Hopefully, something that's sports-related—sports marketing."

Favorite food/meal
"Fruits and vegetables."

My ideal vacation
"Just getting away—being on an island would be really nice."

Hobbies/Other Interests
"Golfing and mountain biking."

If I were not playing football, I'd be a
"Sports marketing representative."

Izell Reese earned the NFL Special Teams Coverage Player of the Year, as selected by the *Dallas Morning News*.

Chef Grady Spears's
CHIHUAHUAN CHORIZO

2 ½ pounds ground pork
1 tablespoon kosher salt
1 teaspoon cracked pepper
6 cloves garlic, minced

8 tablespoons Pasilla Powder (page 142)
1 cup chicken stock
1 cup red wine vinegar

Combine all ingredients thoroughly in a large mixing bowl. Use immediately in a recipe, or divide it into several freezer bags, and store it in the freezer until needed. The chorizo must be cooked before serving.
Yield: about 3 pounds.

GROCERY WORKS.COM ™

What's new and improved at the grocery store? The grocery store.

It's a whole new way to look at grocery shopping. Faster. Easier. Super convenient. Yes, even more - dare we say it? - fun. Find it all at Groceryworks. Your friendly, neighborhood *online* grocer.

www.groceryworks.com

NFL EXPERIENCE
11th year, Atlanta Falcons (5),
San Francisco 49ers (1),
Dallas Cowboys (5)

BIRTHDAY
8-9-67 — *Deion*
1-31-74 — *Pilar*

COLLEGE
Florida State — *Deion*
Syracuse — *Pilar*

PILAR'S OCCUPATION
Model

KIDS
Deiondra (9),
Deion Luwynn, Jr., "Bucky" (5)

PETS
Goodness and Mercy -
Standard Poodles

Deion, Jr., Pilar, Deion, and Deiondra Sanders.

If you could put your own message on a billboard for all to see, what would it be?
"Sooner or later, every knee will bow and every tongue shall confess that Jesus is Lord!" — *Deion*
"Jesus loves you anyway!" — *Pilar*

All children should be taught to
"Adhere to the Ten Commandments." — *Deion*
"Fear the Lord, and the importance of having an honest relationship with God." — *Pilar*

This makes me smile
"Nate Newton and my kids." — *Deion*
"My husband's wit and sense of humor." — *Pilar*

My plans for the future are
"To proclaim the Gospel worldwide." — *Deion*

If you were stranded on a desert island, three things you would take with you
"My Bible, my family, and a boat." — *Deion*
"My Bible, my husband, and water." — *Pilar*

If you could leave one thing behind for the world to learn from life, it would be
"My testimony of how I came to know the Lord." — *Deion*

My hero/heroes are
"My mother is my shero; and T.D. Jakes." — *Deion*
"My mother and father." — *Pilar*

My favorite books/authors are
"The Bible." — *Deion & Pila*

First meal my spouse ever prepared for me
"She made me chicken, rice, and broccoli." — *Deion*
"He hired Chef Anthony." — *Pilar*

Favorite food/meal
"Fried chicken, BBQ baked beans, ox tails, applesauce, and sweet ice tea." — *Deion*
"Pizza, crab claws, and water." — *Pilar*

I wish I could sing like
"Donnie McClurkin." — *Deion*
"Whitney Houston." — *Pilar*

Chef Grady Spears's

DUTCH OVEN POTATOES WITH DRIED FRUIT

2 pounds russet potatoes, scrubbed	kosher salt, to taste
1/2 cup grated Parmesan cheese	freshly-ground black pepper, to taste
2 cups Dried Fruit Mix (recipe follows)	3 tablespoons unsalted butter
2 cups heavy cream	

Preheat the oven to 300 degrees. Use an 8 by 8-inch baking dish, or one of similar size; butter the bottom and sides with 1 tablespoon butter. Wash the potatoes and thinly slice them, using a mandolin, to approximately 1/16-inch thick. If slicing by hand, make the slices paper thin.

Layer one-fifth of the sliced potatoes into the baking dish, making 2 thin layers of potatoes overlapping. Sprinkle with 2 teaspoons of the Parmesan cheese. Top with 1/2 cup fruit, salt, pepper, and 1/2 cup cream. Repeat this step 4 more times, ending with the potatoes. Top the potatoes with the remaining cream and the 3 tablespoons of the butter, cut into small pieces. Sprinkle with the rest of the cheese.

Cover the pan with foil; bake for 2 hours. Uncover the pan; bake for an additional 15 minutes, to lightly brown the top. For a darker brown, place the potatoes under the broiler for a few minutes. Remove the potatoes from the oven; let them sit for 15 minutes before serving.

Cut the potatoes into squares with a sharp knife.

Yield: 6 to 8 servings.

DRIED FRUIT MIXTURE

1/2 cup dried papayas, cut into 1/4-inch dice	1/2 cup raisins
1/2 cup dried pineapples, cut into 1/4-inch dice	1/2 cup dried cranberries

Combine all ingredients; store in an airtight container.

Yield: 2 cups.

My friends call me (nickname)

"Prime Time." — *Deion*

"I call her Baby Girl and Miss P." — *Pilar*

My ideal vacation

"At home with my wife and kids, and fishing." — *Deion*

"Anywhere there is water, sand, and sun." — *Pilar*

Mr. & Mrs. Deion Sanders.

Hobbies/Other Interests

"Fishing and joking." — *Deion*

"Reading." — *Pilar*

I collect

"Biblical literature." — *Deion*

"Fountains and bonsais." — *Pilar*

Deion with his kids.

22

Emmitt SMITH

NFL EXPERIENCE
10th year, Dallas Cowboys

BIRTHDAY
5-15-69

COLLEGE
Florida

Entering the 1999 season, Emmitt already stands
5th in NFL history in rushing yards.

Favorite food/meal
"Breakfast."

Hobbies/Other Interests
"Golf and movies."

If I were not playing football, I'd be a
"State trooper."

In 1998, Emmitt surpassed Tony Dorsett as
the Dallas Cowboys all-time leading rusher.

Chef Grady Spears's
COWBOY BROWNIES

4½ cups (about 1¾ pounds) bittersweet
  chocolate chunks
1 cup unsalted butter, cut into pieces
8 eggs
3 cups sugar
1½ cups flour

½ cup cocoa powder
4 teaspoons vanilla extract
3 cups chopped pecans
1 cup (about 6 ounces) milk chocolate chunks
vanilla ice cream (optional)

Preheat the oven to 325 degrees. Butter a 13 by 9 by 2-inch baking pan; set it aside.

Combine 3 cups (about 1 pound) of the bittersweet chocolate with the butter; melt it in a bowl in the microwave or in a saucepan, over low heat, on the stove. When the butter and chocolate are melted, set aside.

In a mixer, using the paddle attachment, beat the eggs for 3 minutes (on medium speed). Add the sugar; continue to beat, until the mixture is light in color and texture. Add the melted choco-late; combine well. Mix the flour and cocoa together; add them to the chocolate mixture, along with the vanilla. Fold the nuts, the remaining 1½ cups bitter-sweet chocolate chunks, and the milk chocolate chunks into the mixture by hand, or with a mixer, on low speed. Spread the mixture into the prepared pan, using a spatula. Place this pan in a larger pan; pour boiling water halfway up the sides of the larger pan, to create a hot water bath. Place the pans in the oven; bake the mixture for 40 to 45 minutes. Remove the pans from the oven, and remove brownies from the water bath, to allow them to cool. Serve slightly warm, with ice cream, if desired.

In 9 seasons, Emmitt has become one of the all-time great running backs in NFL history.

26

Kevin SMITH

DEFENSIVE BACK • 5' 11" • 190

NFL EXPERIENCE
8th year, Dallas Cowboys

BIRTHDAY
4-7-70

COLLEGE
Texas A&M

KIDS
Kevaughn Rae (6)

PETS
Kohl - Dog

Kevin's confidence, natural ability, consistency, and intelligence have helped him earn the reputation as one of the NFL's most productive cornerbacks.

If you could put your own message on a billboard for all to see, what would it be?
"Peace: May God be with you."

All children should be taught to
"Respect all mankind and nature."

This makes me smile
"A nice spring morning."

If you were stranded on a desert island, three things you would take with you
"Airplane, pilot, and runway."

If you could leave one thing behind for the world to learn from life, it would be
"Always take advantage of the moment."

My plans for the future are
"Own a record label."

My favorite books/authors are
"Anthony de Mello."

Favorite food/meal
"Shrimp Creole."

I wish I could sing like
"Marvin Gaye."

My friends call me (nickname)
"Pup."

My ideal vacation
"Las Vegas."

Hobbies/Other Interests
"Music, fishing, and video games."

I collect
"CDs."

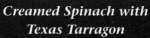

Chef Grady Spears's

CREAMED SPINACH WITH TEXAS TARRAGON

1½ tablespoons unsalted butter
1 cup diced yellow onion
½ teaspoon minced garlic
2 tablespoons fresh Texas tarragon,
   chopped, or 1 teaspoon dried tarragon
1¼ cups heavy cream

⅔ cup (about 2 ounces) grated Parmesan cheese
1 pound cleaned fresh spinach, stems removed and
   well-drained
1 cup fine fresh or dried white bread crumbs
kosher salt, to taste
freshly-ground pepper, to taste

In a large, heavy saucepan, heat the butter (over medium heat). Add the onions, sauté, until they are transparent. Add the garlic; sauté 4 minutes. Add the Texas tarragon; sauté another minute. Add the heavy cream, bring it to a simmer, and stir in the cheese. When the cheese has melted, add the spinach, bread crumbs, salt, and pepper. Stir, to combine all of the ingredients. Cover the pan; let the spinach wilt for 4 minutes. Uncover the pan; cook the spinach an additional 6 minutes, stirring, to blend the spinach and sauce. Serve at once.

   Yield: 5 to 6 servings.

My mother and grandmother, are special because
"They are women in my life—they have helped my growth."

If I were not playing football, I'd be a
"Playing some other sport."

I am thankful my parents/grandparents taught me
"Never give up."

Kevin majored in recreation, parks, and tourism at Texas A&M.

90

Alonzo SPELLMAN

NFL EXPERIENCE
7th year, Chicago Bears (6),
Dallas Cowboys

BIRTHDAY
9-27-71

COLLEGE
Ohio State

Alonzo attended Rancocas Valley (NJ) High—
the same school as Franco Harris.

Chef Grady Spears's
SPICY PECANS

4 cups (about 1 pound) pecan halves
6 tablespoons unsalted butter, melted

4 teaspoons Pasilla Powder (page 142)
$1/2$ cup packed brown sugar

Preheat oven to 350 degrees. In a large bowl, toss the pecans and butter, until all surfaces are coated. Sprinkle the chile powder over the nuts and, again, combine well. Add the sugar; toss, using your hands to keep the sugar from lumping. Dump the entire mixture onto a sheet pan, scraping the residue in the bowl on top of the nuts. Bake the nuts in the oven for 20 minutes, or until the coating on the nuts begins to brown and the sugar melts. The coating, at this point, will not be crunchy, but as the nuts cool, the coating will harden. Store nuts in an airtight container, until needed.

Yield: 4 cups.

53 *Mark* STEPNOSKI

NFL EXPERIENCE
11th year, Dallas Cowboys (7);
Houston/Tennessee Oilers (4)

BIRTHDAY
1-20-67

COLLEGE
Pittsburgh

With girlfriend—Brandi, and Chris Robinson—
singer for the Black Crowes.

If you could put your own message on a billboard for all to see, what would it be?
"Find out things for yourself; don't be a sheep following the rest of the herd."

All children should be taught to
"Respect other people, and have a sense of responsibility."

This makes me smile
"Being around my friends."

If you were stranded on a desert island, three things you would take with you
"A lot of books, solar-powered CD player, and a lot of CDs."

If you could leave one thing behind for the world to learn from life, it would be
"Try to make it a better place for the next guy."

My plans for the future are
"To have the opportunity to compete in the playoffs this year."

My hero is
"Terry Fox."

My favorite books/authors are
"William Greider, Fletcher, Prouty, and Jack Herer."

Favorite food/meal
"Seafood."

I wish I could sing like
"Robert Plant."

My friends call me (nickname)
"Step."

My ideal vacation
"Sydney, Australia, in February."

CORNISH HENS TARRAGON

1¹/₂ cups dry white wine
2 Cornish hens, halved
1 stick butter, melted
1 teaspoon garlic, minced

1¹/₂ teaspoons tarragon
salt and pepper, to taste
paprika, for dusting

Place hens in shallow baking dish. In bowl, combine butter, wine, garlic, tarragon, salt, and pepper. Marinate hens in mixture for 3 hours, or overnight.

Dust with paprika, and place in oven. Bake at 350 degrees for 1¹/₂ hours.

Hobbies/Other Interests
"Reading, travel, music, and finances."

I collect
"Compact discs."

When others describe you, what character qualities do they use?
"Perseverance and generosity."

My mother, is special because
"She has my best interests at heart. "

If I were not playing football, I'd be a
"Road crew member for a musical band."

I am thankful my parents/grandparents taught me
"To be disciplined."

D.J., Mark Tuinei, and Mark
at Steve Beuerlein's wedding.

NFL EXPERIENCE
7th year, Green Bay
Packers (3), Miami Dolphins
(1), Dallas Cowboys (3)

BIRTHDAY
2-18-71 — *George*
5-20-71 — *Consuela*

COLLEGE
Alabama — *George*
Alabama — *Consuela*

KIDS
James II, "J.T." (6), expecting
second child in December

Consuela and J.T. at Disney World.

If you could put your own message on a billboard for all to see, what would it be?
"Everything is NOT always
what it seems." — *George*
"Stay in school." — *Consuela*

All children should be taught to
"Respect their elders." — *George*
"Respect their elders, and
trust in God." — *Consuela*

This makes me smile
"One simple rose." — *Consuela*

If you were stranded on a desert island, three things you would take with you
"Water, cell phone, and food." — *George*
"Water, a book, and food." — *Consuela*

If you could leave one thing behind for the world to learn from life, it would be
"Discipline." — *George*

Our plans for the future are
"To visit Africa." — *George & Consuela*

My hero is
"Martin Luther King, Jr." — *George & Consuela*

My favorite books/authors are
"John Grisham and Maya Angelou." — *Consuela*

First meal my spouse ever prepared for me
"Salisbury steak and rice." — *George*
"Spaghetti." — *Consuela*

Favorite food/meal
"Pepper steak." — *George*
"Pork chops, corn with tomato,
and macaroni." — *Consuela*

I wish I could sing like
"Barry White." — *George*
"My grandmother." — *Consuela*

Chef Grady Spears's
CHORIZO CON QUESO

1 tablespoon corn oil
½ pound Chihuahuan Chorizo (page 116)
½ cup minced white onion
1 clove garlic, minced

1 cup diced tomato
⅓ cup roasted poblano
⅓ cup chicken stock
3 cups grated mild Cheddar

Warm the oil in a heavy saucepan, over medium heat. Add the chorizo; cook it for 2 minutes, or until the fat begins to melt. Add the onion and garlic. Cook, until the chorizo is well-browned. Drain off the grease. Add the tomato, chile, and chicken stock. Bring the mixture to a simmer; slowly add cheese, blending it with a spoon. As each batch of cheese melts, add more, cooking over low heat. When the cheese has melted and the mixture comes together, it is ready to serve. Keep warm while serving.

Yield: 4 cups.

My friends call me (nickname)

"Mr. Glue and Jorge." — *George*

"Suela." — *Consuela*

My ideal vacation

"A week in Maui with Consuela." — *George*

"Secluded island with George." — *Consuela*

Hobbies/Other Interests

"Coin collecting." — *George*

"I like to cook and try different recipes." — *Consuela*

I collect

"Coins." — *George*

"All God's Children ceramics." — *Consuela*

When others describe you, what character qualities do they use?

"Quiet." — *George*

"Head strong." — *Consuela*

My mother, is special because

"She has guided me since birth." — *George*

My mother and grandmother, are special because

"They have taught me about life, and help me with life's experiences." — *Consuela*

If I were not playing football, I'd be a

"Engi

George and J.T. at Disney World
in Orlando.

44 *Robert* THOMAS

RUNNING BACK/LINEBACKER • 6' 1" • 260

NFL EXPERIENCE
2nd year, Dallas Cowboys

BIRTHDAY
12-1-74

COLLEGE
Henderson State

KIDS
Robert L., V (2)

Robert Thomas finished 1998
with 10 special team tackles.

If you could put your own message on a billboard for all to see, what would it be?
"Too blessed to be stressed."

All children should be taught to
"Respect elders, and to strive to be the best they can be."

This makes me smile
"My son."

If you were stranded on a desert island, three things you would take with you
"Bible, PlayStation, and food."

If you could leave one thing behind for the world to learn from life, it would be
"That if you believe in God, you can accomplish anything you set out to do."

My plans for the future are
"To own my own business."

My hero/heroes are
"My parents."

My favorite books/authors are
"The Bible."

Favorite food/meal
"Chili dogs."

I wish I could sing like
"Marvin Gaye."

My friends call me (nickname)
"Red Rock."

My ideal vacation
"To take my family to Disney World."

Hobbies/Other Interests
"Video games, music, and Internet."

When others describe you, what character qualities do they use?
"Warm personality."

Chef Grady Spears's

CACIOTTA CHEESE ENCHILADAS

⅓ cup vegetable oil
8 (8-inch) corn tortillas
2 cups Red Chile Sauce (page 108)

4½ cups (about ¾ pound) grated Caciotta or Monterey Jack cheese

Lightly grease an 11¾ by 7½-inch glass baking pan. Set aside. Heat the oil in a small skillet, over low heat, until it's hot enough to sizzle when a tiny piece of tortilla is dropped in. Using tongs, dip a tortilla into the hot oil, removing it quickly and letting excess oil drip off. Dip tortilla into the chile sauce, and lay it on a flat surface. Sprinkle ½ cup of the cheese down the center of the tortilla, and roll the tortilla from one end to the other. Lay the enchilada in the prepared pan with the seam down. Repeat the steps with each tortilla, fitting them tightly into the pan. Pour the remaining chile sauce over the top of the enchiladas; sprinkle them with the remaining cheese. Prepare these as close to serving time as possible. To finish the enchiladas, preheat the oven to 400 degrees, and bake them for 12 minutes. Serve at once.

Yield: 4 servings.

My mother, is special because

"She always keeps me grounded and is always there for me."

If I were not playing football, I'd be a

"Police officer."

I am thankful my parents/grandparents taught me

"To make Christ the head of my life."

Robert spent the spring of 1999 playing for the Rhein Fire of NFL Europe.

87

Jason TUCKER

WIDE RECEIVER • 6' 1" • 182

NFL EXPERIENCE
Rookie

BIRTHDAY
6-24-76

COLLEGE
TCU

Tucker was a teammate of Chris Brymer
on the NFL Europe team, Rhein Fire.

Chef Grady Spears's
COW CAMP CREAMED CORN

2 cups corn kernels (cut from about 2 ears)
4 slices smoked bacon, diced
¾ cup diced red onion
1 clove garlic, minced
2 cups heavy cream

¾ cup thinly-sliced scallions (about 8 scallions)
¾ cup diced red pepper (about 1 pepper)
kosher salt, to taste
freshly-ground black pepper, to taste

Preheat the oven to 350 degrees. Sauté the diced bacon, over medium heat, using an ovenproof skillet. As the bacon begins to crisp, add the onion and garlic; cook briefly. Add one cup of the corn kernels, stir well, and place the skillet in the 350-degree oven for 10 minutes, to roast the corn.

Remove from the oven, and add the cream. Purée the mixture in a blender; return to a clean saucepan. Add the remaining corn, scallions, and red pepper. Place the saucepan, over medium heat; simmer, until the creamed corn is thickened and reduced to about 3 cups. Stir, to prevent scorching; this will take about 20 minutes. Season with salt and pepper.

Yield: 6 servings.

42 Chris WARREN

RUNNING BACK • 6' 2" • 236

NFL EXPERIENCE
10th year, Seattle Seahawks (8),
Dallas Cowboys (2)

BIRTHDAY
1-24-68

COLLEGE
Ferrum

KIDS
Ariana (7), Kayla (6),
Christopher, III (3), Conlin (2)

Chris with Christopher and Conlin.

If you could put your own message on a billboard for all to see, what would it be?
"Treat others the way you want to be treated."

All children should be taught to
"Do what is right—not what you like."

This makes me smile
"Unity."

If you were stranded on a desert island, three things you would take with you
"Computer, satellite TV, and Paco."

If you could leave one thing behind for the world to learn from life, it would be
"Learning from mistakes makes you a stronger person."

My plans for the future are
"Preparing myself for life after football."

My favorite books/authors are
"Steven King."

Favorite food/meal
"Seafood."

I wish I could sing like
"Marvin Gaye."

My friends call me (nickname)
"C-Dubb, or C."

My ideal vacation
"Two weeks of beach bumming on any tropical island."

Hobbies/Other Interests
"Travel and boxing."

I collect
"Watches."

Chef Grady Spears's
CREAM OF CARROT SOUP

4 carrots, coarsely-chopped
$^1/_2$ onion, coarsely-chopped
4 garlic cloves
$1^1/_2$ cups chicken stock

$2^1/_2$ cups heavy cream
1 teaspoon Pasilla Powder (page 142)
kosher salt, to taste
cracked pepper, to taste

Place the carrots, onion, garlic, and chicken stock in a saucepan.

Bring to a boil; cook for 10 to 15 minutes, or until carrots are tender. Remove from heat; purée in a blender. Place mixture back in a saucepan; add the cream and Pasilla Powder. Simmer, to reduce by one-fourth. Season with salt. Garnish each serving with cracked pepper.

Yield: 4 servings.

When others describe you, what character qualities do they use?

"Laid-back, crazy, and comical."

If I were not playing football, I'd be a

"Computer company CEO."

I am thankful my parents/grandparents taught me

"Respect others."

Kayla, Ariana, and Christopher with Chris.

30 Kenny WHEATON

DEFENSIVE BACK • 5' 10" • 199

NFL EXPERIENCE
3rd year, Dallas Cowboys

BIRTHDAY
3-8-75

COLLEGE
Oregon

Kenny is the first defensive back drafted from the University of Oregon by Dallas since Hall-of-Famer Mel Renfro in 1964.

If you could put your own message on a billboard for all to see, what would it be?
"When you feel you have done all you can do, just 'stand' and be strong."

All children should be taught to
"Respect others."

This makes me smile
"Seeing my family smile."

If you were stranded on a desert island, three things you would take with you
"TV, girlfriend, and family."

If you could leave one thing behind for the world to learn from life, it would be
"It's more to life than 'money' and material things (your family should be first)."

My plans for the future are
"Find peace within myself."

My hero/heroes are
"My two brothers, Robert and Derrek."

Favorite food/meal
"Barbecue."

I wish I could sing like
"G. Levert."

My friends call me (nickname)
"Sweet Wheat."

My ideal vacation
"On a nice, quiet beach."

Hobbies/Other Interests
"Shopping, and TV."

I collect
"Shoes."

When others describe you, what character qualities do they use?
"Good guy, and keeps to himself."

Chef Grady Spears's
CORN-BREAD DRESSING

4 cups crumbled Yaller Bread with Pintos
   (page 92)
2 jalapeño peppers, stemmed and seeded
2 cups diced yellow onion
1 cup diced celery
2 cloves garlic, minced
6 tablespoons unsalted butter

$\frac{1}{3}$ cup chopped pecans (optional)
1 teaspoon dried thyme leaves
kosher salt, to taste
freshly-ground pepper, to taste
3 eggs, lightly-beaten
1 to 1$\frac{1}{4}$ cups chicken stock

Put the crumbled cornbread into a large bowl. Preheat the oven to 325 degrees. Butter an 8 by 8-inch pan; set aside. Mince the jalapeños; set aside. If you have sensitive skin, wear gloves when handling the hot peppers. In a large, heavy skillet, heat the butter, over medium heat. Add the jalapeños, onion, celery, and garlic; sauté, stirring constantly, until the vegetables have softened. Add the pecans, if you're using them, and thyme; season with salt and pepper. Spoon this mixture over the cornbread; toss lightly with a large spoon. Add the egg; toss to blend. Add half the chicken stock; stir, until the mixture is very moist, but short of soupy. Add the remainder, as needed to maintain this consistency. Spoon the dressing into the prepared pan. Bake the dressing for 30 to 40 minutes, or until it sets and the top is lightly-browned.

Cut, and serve hot.

Yield: 6 to 9 servings.

My mother, is special because
"A number of reasons—she is one of a kind."

If I were not playing football, I'd be a
"Some sort of coach."

I am thankful my parents/grandparents taught me
"To love and respect others."

Kenny finished 1998 with 36 tackles.

25
Charlie
WILLIAMS

NFL EXPERIENCE
5th year, Dallas Cowboys

BIRTHDAY
2-2-72

COLLEGE
Bowling Green State

All children should be taught to
"Respect."

My ideal vacation
"Las Vegas."

Hobbies/Other Interests
"Reading comic books."

Charlie Williams finished 1998 with a
career-high 25 defensive tackles.

Chef Grady Spears's
REATA RANCHERO SAUCE

4 cloves garlic, chopped
3 jalapeño peppers, stemmed, seeded, and
    chopped
5 Smoked Tomatoes, chopped (page 83)
1 red onion, chopped

$^1/_4$ cup cilantro leaves
$^1/_2$ cup olive oil
2 cups chicken stock
kosher salt, to taste
freshly-ground pepper, to taste

Combine the garlic, peppers, tomatoes, onion, and cilantro in a food processor. Pulse the motor, to coarsely grind the mixture. In a large, shallow skillet, heat the oil, over medium-high heat. Pour the chopped vegetable mixture into the pan; cook for 5 minutes. Blend in the chicken stock, bring it to a boil, and reduce the heat. Simmer the mixture for about 30 minutes, to reduce and thicken. Season with salt and pepper. Serve at once, or store in the refrigerator. Keeps up to 4 days.

Yield: approximately 3 cups.

ONE FOR A FRIEND

The Cowboys Are
HUNGRY
in '99!

A sure-fire recipe to bring you all the excitement of the Cowboys each season is the *Dallas Cowboys Official Weekly*. To feed your appetite all the facts, figures, and photos (including Cheerleaders), subscribe today.

DALLAS COWBOYS *Official* WEEKLY

One Cowboys Pkwy. • Irving, TX 75063

☐ New Subscription ☐ Renewal (Attach Mailing Label) ☐ Gift
First Class (US Only) and Other Foreign Rates Provided Upon Request
Air Mail to Canada Add $45.00 per year plus 7% G&S Tax
on subscription price only. US Currency
Air Mail to Mexico Add $48.00 per year, US Currency
Please enter my subscription to *Dallas Cowboys Official Weekly*
☐ 1 year (32 issues) for $39.00 ☐ 2 years (64 issues) for $67.00
☐ 3 years (96 issues) for $95.00

Name _____

Address _____

City _____ State _____ Zip +4 _____

☐ #1 Fan Club members deduct 15%. Fan Club Membership No._____
☐ Enclosed find check or money order in the amount of $ _____ made payable to *DALLAS COWBOYS OFFICIAL WEEKLY*.
☐ Charge to my ☐ MasterCard ☐ Visa ☐ Amex   Exp. Date _____

_____
Credit Card Number (Use a dash where there is a space)
Signature _____

Mail a copy of this coupon or call
972 556-9972 for subscription information.
(9 a.m.-5:30 p.m. Central Time, Monday-Friday)

79 *Erik* WILLIAMS

ALL-PRO TACKLE • 6' 6" • 311

NFL EXPERIENCE
9th year, Dallas Cowboys

BIRTHDAY
9-7-68

COLLEGE
Central State (Ohio)

KIDS
Shi (8), Cassius (2)

PETS
Cockatoo

Erik and his children, Cassius and Shi,
relaxing at home (July, 1999).

If you could put your own message on a billboard for all to see, what would it be?
"No more racism."

All children should be taught to
"Respect their parents."

This makes me smile
"When I'm with my children."

If you were stranded on a desert island, three things you would take with you
"Mother, girlfriend, and kids."

My plans for the future are
"To own many food franchises."

My hero/heroes are
"Cassius Clay."

My favorite books/authors are
"*Roots,* by Alex Haley."

Favorite food/meal
"Seafood."

I wish I could sing like
"Luther Vandross."

My friends call me (nickname)
"Big E, Easter"

Erik and his mother at his surprise 30th birthday
party (September, 1998).

Chef Grady Spears's

SOURDOUGH PANCAKES

4 cups bread flour	3 cups milk
1/4 cup sugar	8 tablespoons unsalted butter, melted
2 teaspoons kosher salt	1 1/2 cups sourdough starter (page 163)
2 tablespoons baking powder	2 teaspoons pure vanilla extract
4 eggs	

In a large bowl, sift or combine all of the dry ingredients together. In another bowl, beat the eggs with a whisk. Add the milk, butter, sourdough starter, and vanilla to the eggs. Blend, to combine. Add the liquid ingredients to the dry ingredients, blending with a whisk. Do not overwork the mixture. Heat a lightly-oiled or buttered nonstick flat griddle to medium-high. When the griddle is hot, ladle one-quarter cup of batter onto the griddle; cook for 3 minutes on each side, or until golden brown. Remove finished pancakes to a serving plate. Keep warm, covered, in a 200- degree oven, until serving time. Repeat cooking process until batter is finished.

Yield: 36 pancakes.

My ideal vacation

"Disney World with my children."

Hobbies/Other Interests

"R/C racing."

I collect

"Crystal."

When others describe you, what character qualities do they use?

"Nice and easy going."

My mother, is special because

"She loves the Lord."

If I were not playing football, I'd be a

"High school teacher and coach."

I am thankful my parents/grandparents taught me

"To respect and love people."

Erik and his girlfriend, Chanda, at a concert (March, 1999).

20

Sherman WILLIAMS

RUNNING BACK • 5' 8" • 202

NFL EXPERIENCE
5th year, Dallas Cowboys

BIRTHDAY
8-13-75

COLLEGE
Alabama

KIDS
Sherman, Jr. (9), Kristian (7)

All children should be taught to
"Always have respect for others, and to hope they have respect for you."

My hero/heroes are
"Cassius Clay."

My ideal vacation
"Miami, Florida."

Hobbies/Other Interests
"Shooting pool, and playing cards."

Sherman Williams was first player in Alabama prep history to run for over 3,000 yards in a season with 3,004 yards and 31 touchdowns.

Chef Grady Spears's PASILLA POWDER

5 pasilla chiles

Prepare the pasilla chiles by removing the stem and seeds. Toast the peppers in a skillet (over medium heat) for 5 minutes, turning them frequently, until they are dry and crisp, but not burned. Purée the peppers in a coffee grinder until they become a fine powder.
Yield: 1 cup.

103.7 KVIL

Dallas Cowboys

Catch all the Action with
Brad Sham
&
Babe Laufenberg

Darren & Juli

WOODSON

ALL-PRO DEFENSIVE BACK • 6' 1" • 219

NFL EXPERIENCE
8th year, Dallas Cowboys

BIRTHDAY
4-25-69 — *Darren*
5-22-70 — *Juli*

COLLEGE
Arizona State — *Darren*
North Texas — *Juli*

JULI'S OCCUPATION
Wife and mother

KIDS
DJ (7), Miranda (3)

PETS
Saiko - Akita

Darren, DJ, and Miranda getting ready
to go boating in Florida (June, 1999).

All children should be taught to
"Love God, and to be honest and compassionate towards others." — *Darren & Juli*

This makes me smile
"When I'm with my children." — *Darren*
"When I'm watching my two children playing together." — *Juli*

Our plans for the future are
"To speak fluent in Spanish, and to play a decent game of golf." — *Darren & Juli*

My hero/heroes are
"My parents." — *Juli*

First meal my spouse ever prepared for me
"Tacos, rice, and beans." — *Darren*
"Pork chops and potatoes." — *Juli*

Favorite food/meal
"Soul food, and Juli's tacos." — *Darren*
"Anything chocolate!" — *Juli*

My friends call me (nickname)
"Woody." — *Darren*
"Jules." — *Juli*

My ideal vacation
"Anywhere on the beach with our children." — *Darren & Juli*

Hobbies/Other Interests
"Reading, listening to music, and spending time with my wife and kids." — *Darren*
"Family time, traveling, and decorating my home." — *Juli*

I collect
"CDs." — *Darren*
"Photographs of my children." — *Juli*

Chef Grady Spears's
CHICKEN-FRIED STEAK

FLOUR SPICE
1 1/2 cups flour
2 teaspoons kosher salt
2 teaspoons freshly-ground pepper
4 tablespoons paprika
1/2 cup Shiner Bock, or any good bock beer
2 cups peanut oil

4 tenderized round steaks (about 1/2 pound each)
2 cups Cracked Pepper Gravy (page 68)

BATTER
2 eggs
1/2 cup buttermilk, or 1/4 cup of milk mixed with 1/4 cup Sourdough Starter (page 163)

Prepare the flour spice by blending the flour, salt, pepper, and paprika. Set aside on a plate or wax paper. Prepare the batter by mixing the eggs with a whisk, in a large bowl. Add the buttermilk, or milk and sourdough starter, and beer. Whisk, to blend. Set aside.

In a deep, heavy skillet, heat the oil to 350 degrees. While the oil is heating, prepare the round steaks by dredging them in the flour spice, taking care to coat the meat evenly. Shake off any excess. Dip the meat into the batter and then, again, in the flour spice, evenly coating the batter so it is dry on the outside. When the oil temperature reaches 350 degrees (when a drop of batter sizzles when dropped in it), gently slide one steak into the hot oil. Cook the steak about 5 minutes. Turn it, taking care not to break the coating; cook the meat 5 more minutes, or until the batter is nicely-browned. Drain the cooked steak on paper towels. Repeat with the other steaks. Hold the cooked steaks in a 225-degree oven, until all four are done. Pour Cracked-Pepper Gravy over the steaks, and serve.

DJ, Juli, and Miranda at Lego Land in Florida (June, 1999).

My husband, is special because
"He's the most wonderful father I could ever want for my two beautiful children." — *Juli*

If I were not playing football, I'd be a
"Entrepreneur." — *Darren*

I am thankful my parents/grandparents taught me
"To not be prejudiced." — *Darren & Juli*

DJ and Miranda in Honolulu at Pro Bowl 1999.

93

Peppi ZELLNER

NFL EXPERIENCE
Rookie

BIRTHDAY
3-14-75

COLLEGE
Fort Valley State

Zellner becomes just the second player ever drafted out of Georgia's Fort Valley State by the Cowboys, joining six-time Pro Bowl tackle Rayfield Wright.

Chef Grady Spears's
ANCHO KETCHUP

12 ancho chili peppers, stemmed and seeded
1/2 white onion, diced
5 cloves garlic, minced
6 cups water
5 teaspoons packed brown sugar

2 tablespoons ground cumin
2 cups tomato paste
kosher salt, to taste
freshly-ground pepper, to taste

Place the peppers, onion, and garlic in a large saucepan; cover with the water. Bring to a boil, over high heat; reduce heat, and simmer for about 15 minutes, or until the peppers have absorbed some liquid and have become soft. Remove the peppers, onion, and garlic with a slotted spoon; transfer them to a food processor. Add the brown sugar, cumin, tomato paste, and 1 cup of the liquid that the peppers were cooked in. Purée, adding more pepper liquid, until you reach the desired thickness. Adjust seasonings with salt, pepper, and more brown sugar, if desired. Spoon the ketchup into a glass container. Store it in the refrigerator until ready for use.
Yield: about 5 cups.

More people buy

INTERSTATE BATTERIES

than any other battery.

Joe Gibbs
Owner

Bobby
Labonte
Driver

Jimmy
Makar
*Crew
Chief*

FOR A DEALER NEAR YOU CALL 1-800-CRANK IT

www.interstatebatteries.com

Official
Sponsor

Coaches and Staff

"Any personal contact with an individual member of our organization can help hundreds of people in need. The star on the helmet can move mountains."
— JERRY JONES

Joe & Diann
AVEZZANO

NFL EXPERIENCE
10th year, Dallas Cowboys

BIRTHDAY
11-17-43 — *Joe*
3-10-49 — *Diann*

COLLEGE
Florida State — *Joe*
Patricia Stevens Fashion
Merchandising — *Diann*

DIANN'S OCCUPATION
Small business owner

KIDS
Anthony "Tony" (23)

PETS
Butterscotch - Cat

Joe with friend, Red Steagall, at Cowtown Concert.

If you could put your own message on a billboard for all to see, what would it be?
"Time is precious—let those you care about know it—every day." — *Diann*

All children should be taught to
"Be responsible for their actions, and to be respectful of all people." — *Joe*
"Be kind and respectful." — *Diann*

This makes me smile
"Accomplishing things that make Diann and Tony happy and proud." — *Joe*
"Seeing Joe and Tony happy." — *Diann*

If you were stranded on a desert island, three things you would take with you
"Diann, water, and a fishing pole." — *Joe*
"I would say, Joe, Tony, and the cat—but I wouldn't want them to be stranded!" — *Diann*

If you could leave one thing behind for the world to learn from life, it would be
"Be kind to others." — *Diann*

My plans for the future are
"Keep mind and body moving—don't allow either to get rusty." — *Joe*

My hero/heroes are
"My dad." — *Joe*
"My dad." — *Diann*

My favorite books/authors are
"Lawrence Saunders." — *Diann*

First meal my spouse ever prepared for me
"Steak and corn, all from her farm." — *Joe*
"Pasta." — *Diann*

Favorite food/meal
"Pasta." — *Joe*
"Sushi." — *Diann*

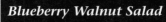

BLUEBERRY WALNUT SALAD

1 bag Italian salad greens
2 cups walnut pieces
1½ cups crumbled Blue cheese

1 small container blueberries
1 bottle raspberry vinaigrette dressing

Clean salad greens, and chill.
Spread walnut pieces on cookie sheet; toast till crispy (not brown).
Clean blueberries.
Just before serving, mix salad greens, blueberries, walnuts, and Blue cheese. Top with salad dressing. Mix, and serve.

I wish I could sing like
"My best friend—country blues artist, Con Hunley." — *Joe*
"Anne Murray." — *Diann*

My friends call me (nickname)
"Avey." — *Joe*

My ideal vacation
"Anywhere with Diann, friends, and music." — *Joe*
"On the beach somewhere with Joe." — *Diann*

Hobbies/Other Interests
"Music." — *Joe*
"Flower arranging, and painting old furniture." — *Diann*

I collect
"Teapots and pitchers." — *Diann*

When others describe you, what character qualities do they use?
"You'll have to ask them—I don't judge; I just do." — *Joe*
"I hope, kindness and caring." — *Diann*

My wife, is special because
"She is the kindest person I have ever met." — *Joe*

Diann and Tony Avezzano enjoying time together at Special Olympics event.

Tony Avezzano enjoying pre-game his last basketball season at Midwestern State.

My husband, is special because
"His love has sustained me through good times and bad times." — *Diann*

I am thankful my parents/ grandparents taught me
"Respect of all people and work ethic." — *Joe*
"The importance of family." — *Diann*

151

Bill & Denise
BATES

NFL EXPERIENCE
2nd year, Dallas Cowboys

BIRTHDAY
6-6-61 — *Bill*
1-25-60 — *Denise*

COLLEGE
Tennessee — *Bill*
Tennessee — *Denise*

DENISE'S OCCUPATION
Mom

KIDS
Graham, Brianna,
and Hunter (10), Tanner (8),
Dillon (4)

PETS
Batgirl & Ginger
Spice - gerbils; fish

152

Mother of the Year Luncheon—April, 1999.

If you could put your own message on a billboard for all to see, what would it be?

"Trust in the Lord." — *Bill*

"Parental complacency is the greatest danger to your child." — *Denise*

All children should be taught to

"Take their plates back to the kitchen!" — *Bill*

"Love God, respect their parents, and good manners." — *Denise*

This makes me smile

"Having made someone else happy! Also, playing golf!" — *Bill*

"Watching my children play." — *Denise*

If you were stranded on a desert island, three things you would take with you

"My wife, Oreo's, and a football." — *Bill*

"A good book, my camera, and my husband." — *Denise*

If you could leave one thing behind for the world to learn from life, it would be

"Love a child." — *Bill*

"Practice random acts of kindness." — *Denise*

Our plans for the future are

"Live each day to the fullest, and attend as many of our children's events as possible." — *Bill & Denise*

My hero/heroes are

"Jack Nicklaus." — *Bill*

"My husband, and the strong women in my family—my mother and my grandmother." — *Denise*

My favorite books/authors are

"*A Good Walk Spoiled.*" — *Bill*

"Last book I read was *The Divine Secrets of the YaYa Sisterhood.*" — *Denise*

First meal my spouse ever prepared for me

"Lasagna . . . and hasn't cooked since!" — *Denise*

Favorite food/meal

"Denise's chicken stroganoff." — *Bill*

"Anything Italian, or lamb chops." — *Denise*

MOTHER PEGGY'S CHICKEN CASSEROLE

2 cans cream of chicken soup
3 or 4 chicken breasts and several thighs
1 bag Pepperidge Farm Stuffing Mix

1 egg
cheese, optional

Stew 3 or 4 chicken breasts and thighs; remove meat from bones. Mix 2 cans cream of chicken soup with 1 can water. Mix bag of stuffing with 1 egg and chicken broth, until soft.

In a casserole dish, layer bottom with chicken pieces, cover with soup mixture, and put dressing mixture on top. You can add 2 cups rice to the soup.

Cook, covered with foil, at 375 degrees for 45 minutes. May sprinkle grated cheese on top.

CHEESY POTATOES

1 2-pound bag frozen hash brown potatoes, thawed
1 medium onion, chopped
salt and pepper, to taste
1¼ sticks margarine

1 10¾-ounce can undiluted cream of chicken soup
8 ounces American process cheese
1 8-ounce container sour cream
1½ cups cornflakes, crushed

Spread hash browns in a 9x13-inch baking dish. Sprinkle with onion, salt, and pepper. Melt margarine; pour half over potatoes (reserve remaining margarine for topping).

Heat soup and cheese in a medium saucepan, stirring, until cheese is melted. Mix in sour cream; pour mixture over potatoes. Combine crushed cornflakes and reserved margarine; sprinkle evenly over top of casserole. Bake at 350 degrees for 1 hour.

I wish I could sing like
"Elton John." — *Bill*
"Whitney Houston." — *Denise*

My friends call me (nickname)
"Billybob or Billygoat." — *Bill*
"Necie or Nene." — *Denise*

My ideal vacation
"Three weeks in Europe." — *Bill*
"A tropical island or Europe." — *Denise*

The Bates family—Easter, 1999.

Hobbies/Other Interests
"Golf, fishing, skiing, tennis, canoeing, rafting, baseball, basketball, i.e., anything sports-related!" — *Bill*

"Gardening, photography, and scrapbooking." — *Denise*

I collect
"Golf clubs." — *Bill*
"Teapots." — *Denise*

When others describe you, what character qualities do they use?
"Intense." — *Bill*
"An organizer and leader." — *Denise*

My wife, is special because
"Denise is a wonderful wife who cares for our busy family's every need. I hate leaving her and, when I am gone, I cannot wait to be with her again, because she makes everyday special." — *Bill*

153

NFL EXPERIENCE
9th year, Cleveland Browns (4), Atlanta Falcons (1), Dallas Cowboys (4)

BIRTHDAY
5-31-46 — *Jim*
9-4-46 — *Beverly*

COLLEGE
Tennessee — *Jim*
UCLA — *Beverly*

BEVERLY'S OCCUPATION
Fashion coordinator

KIDS
James, Jr. (26), Jeremy (23)

GRANDKIDS
Jake

James, Jake, and Tina Bates.

Jim and Beverly Bates.

JALAPEÑO-CITRUS TUNA STEAKS

3 tablespoons olive oil
2 tablespoons finely-chopped fresh oregano
$1/2$ teaspoon cayenne pepper
1 teaspoon kosher salt
4 (7- to 8-ounce) ahi tuna steaks, each 1-inch thick

4 small oranges, about 6 ounces each
1 lime
1 teaspoon honey
1 jalapeño chili, seeded and minced
1 teaspoon red pepper flakes
$1/8$ teaspoon ground cumin

Mix together the olive oil, oregano, cayenne pepper, and salt, in a small bowl. Brush mixture over both sides of the tuna steaks. Cover with plastic wrap; marinate in the refrigerator at least 15 minutes, or as long as 45 minutes.

Grill the tuna steaks, over medium heat, turning once (4 minutes for rare, or as long as 8 minutes for well-done). Serve warm with citrus relish.

RELISH: Cut the skin and outer white pith from the oranges, with a sharp knife. Slide the knife down one side of each orange segment; then, down the other side, removing the segments as you go. Cut the segments into $1/2$-inch pieces; place them in a bowl. Follow the same procedure for the lime; combine the orange and lime pieces. Add the honey, jalapeño, red pepper flakes, and cumin. Stir and toss, to mix well. Set aside.

Yield: 4 servings.

BLACKWELL

VIDEO DIRECTOR

NFL EXPERIENCE
19th year, Dallas Cowboys

BIRTHDAY
12-1-50 — *Robert*
5-25-58 — *Diana*

COLLEGE
Stephen F. Austin — *Robert*
California Lutheran — *Diana*

DIANA'S OCCUPATION
Flight attendant for
American Airlines

KIDS
Nate (12), Lora (5)

PETS
Lady - 7-year-old Sheltie

The Blackwells—Diana, Robert, Lora, and Nate
(Christmas, 1998).

If you could put your own message on a billboard for all to see, what would it be?
"If it was easy, everybody would do it." — *Robert*
"Don't sweat the small stuff." — *Diana*

All children should be taught to
"Set goals in life and strive
to reach them." — *Robert*
"Be respectful to others." — *Diana*

This makes me smile
"Watching my children grow older." — *Robert*
"Good friendships." — *Diana*

Our plans for the future are
"Retire and travel
(without the kids)." — *Robert & Diana*

If you were stranded on a desert island, three things you would take with you
"Picture of my family, sunglasses,
and a blender." — *Robert*
"Sunscreen, cell phone, and
'People' magazine." — *Diana*

If you could leave one thing behind f or the world to learn from life, it would be
"Don't be so serious; relax,
and enjoy life!" — *Robert*
"Enjoy the music!" — *Diana*

My hero/heroes are
"Glen Blackwell, my father." — *Robert*
"The unsung heroes of our daily lives." — *Diana*

Nate and Robert Blackwell at the 1999 NFL Draft in
Madison Square Garden, New York City (April 18, 1999).

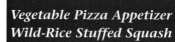

Robert & Diana Blackwell

**Vegetable Pizza Appetizer
Wild-Rice Stuffed Squash**

VEGETABLE PIZZA APPETIZER

2 cans crescent rolls
12-ounce package of cream cheese
$^1/_2$ cup mayonnaise
$^1/_2$ teaspoon dillweed
$^1/_2$ teaspoon dry minced onion
1 package dry Ranch Dressing Mix

$^1/_3$ cup broccoli
$^1/_3$ cup mushrooms
$^1/_3$ cup cauliflower
$^1/_3$ cup red onion
$^1/_3$ cup red pepper
$^1/_3$ cup green pepper

Preheat oven to 400 degrees. Spread crescent rolls on a cookie sheet. Bake for 8-10 minutes; then, cool. *(Can be done the night before.)* Mix cream cheese, mayonnaise, dillweed, dry minced onion, and dry Ranch mix. Spread evenly over crescent rolls.

Dice broccoli, mushrooms, cauliflower, red onion, red pepper, and green pepper. Mix together in a ziplock bag; apply to top of Ranch dressing mixture. Pat it down on top of mixture.

Cut into bite-size squares, and serve.

WILD RICE-STUFFED SQUASH

2 cans (14$^1/_2$-ounce) reduced-sodium chicken
  broth
1 teaspoon dried thyme, crushed
$^2/_3$ cup wild rice, rinsed
$^1/_2$ pound leeks, green parts removed, ends
  trimmed, chopped (1 cup)
$^2/_3$ cup long grain rice
12 small winter squash (such as Acorn, Sweet
  Dumpling, or Golden Nugget), each about
  3$^1/_2$ to 4 inches in diameter

$^1/_2$ cup dried cranberries or dried currants
$^1/_2$ cup dried apricots, snipped
6 tablespoons margarine or butter, melted
$^1/_4$ teaspoon salt
$^1/_4$ teaspoon pepper
fresh sage leaves (optional)

Bring chicken broth and thyme to boiling in a large saucepan. Add uncooked wild rice; reduce heat. Cook, covered, for 30 minutes. Add leeks and uncooked long grain rice. Cover, and simmer 15 minutes more, or till rice is tender. Let stand, covered, for 5 minutes. Drain excess liquid, if necessary.

Wash squash. Cut off top third, including the stem end, from each. Scrape out seeds with a spoon. Place squash, cut sides down, in a shallow baking pan. Bake in a 350-degree oven for 30 minutes. Turn cut sides up. Cover pan with foil; bake about 20 minutes more, or till tender. Remove from oven; set aside.

Stir rice mixture, dried cranberries or currants, and dried apricots together in a large bowl. Stir in melted margarine or butter, salt, and pepper.

Mound stuffing into squash. Place in a shallow baking pan. Bake in a 425-degree oven about 10 minutes, or till heated through. Garnish with sage leaves, if desired. Makes 12 side-dish servings.

Tɪᴘ: Prepare up to the point where squash is stuffed; refrigerate, covered, up to 1 day. To serve, bring to room temperature and bake, as directed.

My wife, is special because
"She keeps the household organized and the family together during the football season, when I can't be home very much." — *Robert*

My husband, is special because
"He puts up with me." — *Diana*

I am thankful my parents/grandparents taught me
"That you have to work for what you want out of life." — *Robert*
"To work hard and play hard." — *Diana*

My friends call me (nickname)
"Often." — *Diana*

BROWN

NFL EXPERIENCE
8th year, Miami Dolphins (4),
Dallas Cowboys (4)

BIRTHDAY
7-6-64 — *Britt*
6-7-67 — *Laura*

COLLEGE
TCU — *Britt*
TCU — *Laura*

LAURA'S OCCUPATION
Medical Transcriptionist/Mom

KIDS
Chase (5), Sydney (3),
Payton (1)

The Brown family.

All children should be taught to
"Respect authority." — *Britt*
"Respect other people." — *Laura*

This makes me smile
"My kids; and players we've rehabed return to playing successfully." — *Britt*
"Seeing Britt and the kids playing together." — *Laura*

If you were stranded on a desert island, three things you would take with you
"Laura, golf bag with clubs, and a set of dumbells." — *Britt*
"Toothbrush, swimsuit, and radio." — *Laura*

Our plans for the future are
"To retire in Lampasas, Texas." — *Britt & Laura*

My favorite books/authors are
"John Grisham, Sidney Sheldon, and Danielle Steele." — *Laura*

First meal my spouse ever prepared for me
"Shrimp and rice casserole." — *Britt*
"Lemon pepper chicken." — *Laura*

Favorite food/meal
"Rib eye steak, and roast on Sundays." — *Britt*
"Mexican food." — *Laura*

I wish I could sing like
"George Strait." — *Britt*
"Celine Dion." — *Laura*

Laura and Britt Brown skiing in Colorado with good friend, Brad Escoe.

158

SALSA

4-5 tomatoes, cut up in large pieces
1 bunch green onions
1 bunch cilantro
1-2 jalapeño peppers
1 lime
1 small can black olives, chopped
salt

In food processor, mix green onions, peppers, and cilantro. Set aside.

In blender, blend tomatoes, until smooth. Add juice of 1 lime, green onion mixture, and black olives. Blend. Add salt, to taste. Can add more fresh tomatoes, or even a can of tomatoes, if too hot. Cilantro makes this tasty!

SHEPHERD'S PIE

round Hawaiian loaf bread—middle cut out and cubed
8 ounces cream cheese
2 cups sour cream
1 jar dried beef, cut up
3-4 green onions, chopped
1 tablespoon Worchesterhire sauce
1 package grated Cheddar cheese

Cut out bread (make a lid). Mix all other ingredients, and fill bread with it. Bake in 350-degree oven for 1 hour. Great appetizer!

My friends call me (nickname)
"Jakie." — *Britt*

My ideal vacation
"Sun, golf, and sleep (naps)." — *Britt*
"One month at a beach resort, alternating weeks with and without the kids." — *Laura*

Hobbies/Other Interests
"Weight training and golf." — *Britt*
"Working out, shopping, and reading." — *Laura*

I collect
"Nutritional supplements." — *Britt*
"Books." — *Laura*

When others describe you, what character qualities do they use?
"Aggressiveness, sarcastic humor, caring, and confident." — *Britt*
"Organized, sensitive, and conservative." — *Laura*

My wife, is special because
"She is very real—'no hidden agenda'; with 3 kids, she is organized!!" — *Britt*

I am thankful my parents/grandparents taught me
"Respect for others." — *Britt*
"The Golden Rule: 'Do unto others as you would have done unto you.'" — *Laura*

Sydney, Chase, and Payton Brown.

Bucky & Amy
BUCHANAN

NFL EXPERIENCE
6th year, Dallas Cowboys

BIRTHDAY
6-9-61 — Bucky
4-3-65 — Amy

AMY'S OCCUPATION
Administrative Assistant—EDS

KIDS
Thomas (12), Brett (9)

PETS
Barney - Cocker Spaniel

Amy, Bucky, Brett, and Thomas Buchanan.

All children should be taught to

"Be respectful and responsible." — *Bucky*

"Know the Lord—all the rest
falls into place." — *Amy*

This makes me smile

"A good day of golf." — *Bucky*

"Watching my children accomplish a new goal;
sitting by a pool with friends relaxing." — *Amy*

If you could leave one thing behind for the world to learn from life, it would be

"A responsible, respectful,
and loving child." — *Bucky & Amy*

My hero/heroes are

"My father, Big Buck Buchanan." — *Bucky*

Favorite food/meal

"Steak, Tex-Mex, and junk food." — *Bucky*

"Seafood, steak, and chocolate-chip
ice cream." — *Amy*

My ideal vacation

"On the beach." — *Bucky*

"Two full weeks on a beach
(any beach) with my family!!" — *Amy*

Hobbies/Other Interests

"Golf, working around the house, and playing
any sport with my sons." — *Bucky*

"Fishing, reading, and relaxing." — *Amy*

I collect

"Baseball hats." — *Bucky*

"Dickens Christmas houses." — *Amy*

When others describe you, what character qualities do they use?

"Generous, fun loving, honest,
and stubborn." — *Bucky*

"Good listener, outgoing, devoted,
and ornery." — *Amy*

PECAN TASSIES

1 package (3-ounce) cream cheese
1/2 cup margarine
1 cup flour
2 eggs
1 cup brown sugar

1 tablespoon soft margarine
1 teaspoon vanilla
1/4 cup light syrup
2/3 cup pecans

Mix cream cheese, margarine, and flour together. Make dough into balls, and pat each around the edges of a small, greased muffin pan. Mix remaining ingredients; pour over the dough.
Bake at 325 degrees for 25 minutes.

CHOCOLATE-CHEESE COOKIES

2 rolls slice-and-bake chocolate-chip cookies*
1 package (8-ounce) cream cheese
1/4 cup sugar

1 egg
1 teaspoon vanilla

In a jelly roll pan, press one roll of the cookies—that has been allowed to warm to room temperature—into the bottom of the pan. Mix cream cheese, sugar, egg, and vanilla; spread over cookie dough. Slice the second roll of cookie dough thinly; place on top of cream cheese filling.
Bake at 350 degrees for 25 to 30 minutes. Cut into bars.
*Freeze one roll, and let the other one come to room temperature.

My mother, is special because

"She taught me how to be a good mother with discipline, love, and a sense of humor—love you, Mom!" — *Amy*

Thomas and Brett Buchanan.

Dave & Kay
CAMPO

NFL EXPERIENCE
11th year, Dallas Cowboys

BIRTHDAY
7-18-47 — *Dave*
7-22-56 — *Kay*

COLLEGE
Central Connecticut State;
Albany State — *Dave*
Stevens Henniger Business
School — *Kay*

KAY'S OCCUPATION
Homemaker

KIDS
Angie (24), Eric (23), Becky
(21), Tommy (19), Shelbie (18),
Michael (8)

GRANDKIDS
Aubrey (4), Madyson (4)

Dave and Kay, with Kay's sisters
and their husbands on a Caribbean cruise.

If you could put your own message on a billboard for all to see, what would it be?
"Strive to be the best." — *Dave*

All children should be taught to
"Have faith in God, and believe in themselves."
— *Dave*
"Respect people." — *Kay*

This makes me smile
"My son Michael's personality." — *Dave*

If you were stranded on a desert island, three things you would take with you
"Guitar, Bible, and CD player with lots of CDs and batteries." — *Dave*

If you can leave one thing behind for the world to learn from life, it would be
"Treat people as you would like to be treated." — *Dave*

My hero/heroes are
"Sports—Frank Gifford;
Personal—my dad." — *Dave*

My favorite books/authors are
"Anything by Tom Clancy." — *Dave*
"John Grisham." — *Kay*

First meal my spouse ever prepared for me
"Pasta." — *Dave*

Favorite food/meal
"Grandma Campo's spaghetti." — *Dave*
"Sweets." — *Kay*

Eric, Angie and Shelbie, with Kay and
Dave at Angie's college graduation.

CHICKEN TORTILLA SOUP

vegetable oil (for deep frying)
8 corn tortillas or more, sliced thinly
1 small onion, finely chopped
2 large fresh garlic cloves, minced
1 tablespoon chili powder
2 teaspoons ground cumin
1/2 teaspoon dried oregano
1 bay leaf
6 cups chicken stock or low salt canned broth
1 8-ounce can tomato sauce
1 teaspoon sugar

1/4 teaspoon pepper
2 large chicken breasts
1 1/2 cups corn, or 2 ears corn

TOPPINGS:
sour cream
cilantro
red onion
avacado
Monterey Jack cheese

Fry tortilla strips in hot oil, until crisp; drain. Transfer 1 tablespoon oil to a large pot; add onion and sauté, over medium heat, until tender (about 5 minutes). Add garlic, chili powder, cumin, oregano, and bay leaf; sauté 1 minute. Add broth, tomato sauce, sugar, and pepper; boil. Add chicken. Cover pot and simmer until chicken is just cooked through (about 15 minutes).

Transfer chicken to plate; cool, and chop. Add corn. Simmer until corn is tender (about 5 minutes). Serve with tortilla strips and other toppings.

This can be prepared one day ahead; cover and refrigerate.

BUTTERFLY SHRIMP IN THE OVEN

30 fresh large shrimp, remove tails
1/4 cup olive oil
3/4 cup bread crumbs
pinch of salt, pepper, and crushed red pepper
2 large fresh garlic cloves, minced

10 parsley psrings, chopped
6 tablespoons butter, melted
1/4 cup grated Parmesan cheese

Arrange shrimp in a 10x13-inch baking dish. Pour olive oil on top. Sprinkle with bread crumbs, garlic, and parsley; stir. Cover with foil and bake at 300 degrees for 20 minutes. Pour butter over shrimp; sprinkle with cheese. Bake uncovered for 5 minutes.

I wish I could sing like

"Luther Vandross." — *Dave*

My friends call me (nickname)

"Camps." — *Dave*

My ideal vacation

"Caribbean Islands." — *Dave*

"Cruising anywhere." — *Kay*

Michael and Rowdy
at the Christmas Party.

Hobbies/Other Interests

"Music, watching sports, and golf." — *Dave*

"Scrapbooks, and crafts." — *Kay*

I collect

"Hats (sports)." — Dave

"Lladro, Chararchi crystal, and Estée Lauder small bottle collection." — Kay

When others describe you, what character qualities do they use?

"Humorous, and competitive." — Dave

Blake CUNDIFF

ASSISTANT STRENGTH AND CONDITIONING

NFL EXPERIENCE
3rd year, Dallas Cowboys

BIRTHDAY
8-13-57

COLLEGE
North Texas

If you could put your own message on a billboard for all to see, what would it be?
"Good things happen to good people."

All children should be taught to
"Believe in a higher power, and to respect their parents."

My plans for the future are
"To continue to have an impact on the lives of others."

My hero/heroes are
"My parents and grandparents."

My favorite books/authors are
"*Tales from Margaritaville,* by Jimmy Buffett."

Favorite food/meal
"Any kind of seafood."

I wish I could sing like
"Anybody else—I can't sing at all."

My friends call me (nickname)
"Bam Bam."

My ideal vacation
"Anyplace in the Rocky Mountains with a fly rod in my hand."

Hobbies/Other Interests
"Fly fishing, snow skiing, and riding Harleys."

When others describe you, what character qualities do they use?
"Trustworthy, strong willed, easy to get along with, and friendly."

I am thankful my parents/grandparents taught me
"The importance of a good education."

Chef Grady Spears's MOLASSES RUB

1 cup packed light brown sugar
2 tablespoons molasses
1 1/2 teaspoons kosher salt
2 teaspoons paprika

1 1/2 teaspoons freshly-ground pepper
2 teaspoons dried thyme leaves
1 teaspoon garlic powder

Combine the ingredients in the bowl of a food processor and process, until the mixture is well-blended. Remove the rub, and use it as needed, or store it in an airtight container.

Rich & Ros
DALRYMPLE

DIRECTOR OF PUBLIC RELATIONS

NFL EXPERIENCE
10th year, Dallas Cowboys

BIRTHDAY
8-2-60 — *Rich*
1-10-64 — *Ros*

COLLEGE
Westminster College -
Pennsylvania — *Rich*
Miami (FL) — *Ros*

ROS'S OCCUPATION
Homemaker

KIDS
Kimberley (8), Clayton (6),
Ty and Jack (1)

PETS
Tropical fish

Mom, Kim, Ty, Clay, Jack, and Dad.

All children should be taught to
"Respect and listen to their parents." — *Rich*
"Be responsible." — *Ros*

This makes me smile
"Having my kids greet me at
my car when I come home from work." — *Rich*
"Our four children playing
on the beach." — *Ros*

If you were stranded on a desert island, three things you would take with you
"Lots of magazines to read, a case
of Mountain Dew, and sunblock." — *Rich*
"Matches, beer, and spam—so I could enjoy a small
vacation, and then return home." — *Ros*

If you could leave one thing behind for the world to learn from life, it would be
"Make the most of any opportunity
you have." — *Rich*
"Mind over matter. You can do it,
if you try, try, try." — *Ros*

Our plans for the future are
"Create a loving and fun household
for our children to grow up in,
so that they'll always come back." — *Rich & Ros*

Jack (left), Mom, and Ty (right) taking a
moment before bed.

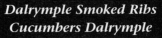

DALRYMPLE SMOKED RIBS

4-5 pounds pork loin ribs, or spare ribs
1 bottle of your favorite BBQ sauce

honey, to taste *(the kids love this taste!)*

Mix BBQ sauce and honey to your family's taste. Let the kids "paint" the ribs with the marinate; marinate overnight.

Stoke up the smoker; smoke ribs 45 minutes per pound. Remove, and wrap with foil. Place wrapped ribs in a brown bag. This helps them "rest" and obtain that restaurant quality! Let them rest for about an hour, and cut off individual ribs with kitchen scissors. (Can also be done on BBQ grill.)

CUCUMBERS DALRYMPLE

cucumbers
onions
1/2 cup vinegar

3 tablespoons water
salt and pepper
sugar, to taste

Slice cucumbers and onions in whatever proportions you want. Mix marinate, according to taste; combine with cucumbers and onions. Chill. Serve with ribs around the pool, and you'll be amazed at how much you can eat!

Kim, Clay, and Ros at a picnic in Grapevine Springs Park in Coppell.

My hero/heroes are
"Roberto Clemente and Art Rooney." — *Rich*
"Princess Diana." — *Ros*

My favorite books/authors are
"Dan Jenkins." — *Rich*
"Usually any bestseller." — *Ros*

First meal my spouse ever prepared for me
"Spaghetti." — *Rich*
"Pancakes." — *Ros*

Favorite food/meal
"Chicken fajitas." — *Rich*
"Smoked ribs and salad around the pool." — *Ros*

I wish I could sing like
"Jackson Browne." — *Rich*
"Barry White and Vanda Shepard." — *Ros*

My friends call me (nickname)
"Rich." — *Rich*
"Bud." — *Ros*

My ideal vacation
"Sun, water, and cable TV." — *Rich*
"Anywhere near a good beach with kid-friendly activities close by." — *Ros*

Hobbies/Other Interests
"Running, and working on the house." — *Rich*
"Raising children, tennis, golf, and jogging." — *Ros*

George & Jami
EDWARDS

NFL EXPERIENCE
2nd year, Dallas Cowboys

BIRTHDAY
1-16-67 — *George*
3-20-69 — *Jami*

COLLEGE
Duke — *George*

JAMI'S OCCUPATION
Accountant

Jami and George Edwards.

If you could put your own message on a billboard for all to see, what would it be?
"Respect others . . . and they will respect you." —*Jami*

All children should be taught to
"Be pragmatic." — *George*
"Read, write, and respect others." — *Jami*

This makes me smile
"Fulfillment and success." —*George*
"When the Cowboys are winning." — *Jami*

If you could leave one thing behind for the world to learn from life, it would be
"Control the things that you can control, and pray for the things you cannot control." — *George*

Our plans for the future are
"Become successful professionals, and start a family." — *George & Jami*

My hero/heroes are
"Jesus Christ." — *George*

My favorite books/authors are
"*On Waldon Pond,* by Henry David Thoreau." — *George*
"Stuart Woods and John Grisham." — *Jami*

First meal my spouse ever prepared for me
"Steak." — *George*
"BBQ ribs." — *Jami*

Favorite food/meal
"Fried chicken." — *George*
"Lobster." — *Jami*

I wish I could sing like
"Luther Vandross." — *George*
"Whitney Houston." — *Jami*

SEAFOOD STEW

28-ounce can (3 cups) tomatoes, undrained and cut-up
16-ounce (2 cups) stewed tomatoes, undrained and cut-up
8-ounce can (1 cup) tomato sauce
1 cup dry wine
2 teaspoons basil leaves
1 teaspoon salt
1/4 teaspoon pepper
12 small clams, washed
1/3 cup oil

1 1/2 cups chopped onions
1 cup chopped fresh parsley
1 pound fresh, medium shrimp, shelled, and deveined
6 garlic cloves, minced
1 pound frozen crab legs, in shells, thawed, and cracked
1 pound fresh fish, cut into 1 1/2-inch pieces
loaf of French bread
hot sauce, to taste

In a large pot, combine all tomatoes and sauce, wine, basil, salt, and pepper. Bring to boil. Simmer, uncovered, for 10 minutes, stirring occasionally. Bring back to boil; add clams. Cover; cook, until clams open (about 4-6 minutes).

In medium sauce pan, heat oil. Stir in onions, parsley, shrimp, and garlic. Simmer, covered, for 3-5 minutes, or until shrimp are slightly-pink. Stir into large pot with tomatoes and clams; add crab. Simmer, uncovered, for 5 minutes. Add fish; cook for 2-3 minutes, or until fish flakes.

Serve with thick slices of French bread, to dip in broth.

PEACH HALVES WITH RASPBERRY SAUCE

2 teaspoons cornstarch
1/2 cup currant jelly
10-ounce package frozen raspberries, thawed and drained

6 fresh peach halves
1 quart (4 cups) vanilla ice cream

In medium sauce pan, combine cornstarch, jelly, and raspberries. Cook, until thick, over medium heat. Let cool.

Place one peach half in each dish (6). Top with a scoop of ice cream, and spoon cooled raspberry sauce over ice cream.

My ideal vacation
"Traveling with family." — *George*
"Any quiet island in the Caribbean." — *Jami*

Hobbies/Other Interests
"Exercise, reading, and fishing." — *George*
"Art, reading, and cooking." — *Jami*

I collect
"Lladro statues." — *Jami*

My wife, is special because
"I would not be where
I am without her." — *George*

My husband, is special because
"He is very caring, giving, and makes me smile." — *Jami*

I am thankful my parents/ grandparents taught me
"A good work ethic." — *George*

169

Buddy & Jere GEIS

QUARTERBACKS

NFL EXPERIENCE
8th year, Green Bay Packers
(5), Indianapolis Colts (2),
Dallas Cowboys (1)

BIRTHDAY
9-16-46 — *Buddy*
5-31-49 — *Jere*

COLLEGE
Lock Haven, Arizona — *Buddy*
Arizona — *Jere*

KIDS
Adam (24), Jeni (20)

PETS
Carl - Rottweiler

Buddy and Jere Geis at Cowboys Christmas Party.

If you could put your own message on a billboard for all to see, what would it be?
"Congratulations, Dallas Cowboys: New Millennium Super Bowl Champions!" — *Buddy*
"It takes both rain and sunshine to make a rainbow." — *Jere*

All children should be taught to
"Respect their elders." — *Buddy*
"Believe in themselves." — *Jere*

This makes me smile
"Life." — *Buddy*
"Happy 'endings.'" — *Jere*

If you were stranded on a desert island, three things you would take with you
"Jere, Adam, and Jeni." — *Buddy*
"Buddy, books, and a box of flares." — *Jere*

If you could leave one thing behind for the world to learn from life, it would be
"Never hate; always maintain a positive mental attitude." — *Buddy*
"Don't sweat the small stuff." — *Jere*

Our plans for the future are
"To show off my Dallas Cowboys Super Bowl Ring! A healthy, happy retirement on the beach." — *Buddy & Jere*

My hero/heroes are
"Our families." — *Buddy & Jere*

My favorite books/authors are
"*The Godfather,* by Mario Puzzo." — *Buddy*
"John Grisham." — *Jere*

First meal my spouse ever prepared for me
"Kraft macaroni and cheese." — *Buddy*
"I'm still waiting." — *Jere*

Favorite food/meal
"Italian." — *Buddy*
"Pizza, and chocolate." — *Jere*

40th Anniversary

BARBECUED SHRIMP

8-10 pounds jumbo shrimp*
1 pound butter
1 pound margarine
6 ounces Worcestershire
6 tablespoons finely-ground black pepper
   (I use 4!)

1 teaspoon ground rosemary
2 lemons, thinly-sliced
   (remove seeds, and toss in)
1 teaspoon Tabasco sauce *(I use ¹/₂!)*
4 teaspoons salt
¹/₂ teaspoon garlic powder

DAY BEFORE: melt butter and margarine, add remaining ingredients, and mix thoroughly. Bring to a boil for a couple of minutes; then, let simmer. Put in refrigerator.

NEXT DAY: reheat.

Place shrimp in two-9x13-inch pans *(don't pile too thick)*. Pour sauce over top; toss, to cover.

Bake at 400 degrees for 15-20 minutes. Turn at 8 minutes. Shells are pink.

Serve with French bread, to dip into the "barbeque" sauce (a New Orleans must!).

If you use 10 pounds, you might want to 1¹/₂ times the recipe. Figure ³/₄ pound per person, or 20 shrimp per pound.

I wish I could sing like

"Julio Iglesias." — *Buddy*

"Celine Dion." — *Jere*

My ideal vacation

"Neptune Beach, Florida." — *Buddy & Jere*

Hobbies/Other Interests

"Running, tennis, and Special Olympics volunteer." — *Buddy*

I collect

"Cologne!" — *Buddy*

"Annalee dolls." — *Jere*

Adam and Buddy.

When others describe you, what character qualities do they use?

"Optimistic and enthusiastic." — *Buddy*

My wife, is special because

"She always has faith in me." — *Buddy*

If I were not playing football, I'd be a

"Special needs teacher/counselor." — *Buddy*

Jeni with Carl.

Bob & Emily HAAS

NFL EXPERIENCE
6th year, Dallas Cowboys

BIRTHDAY
5-7-69 —Bob
6-3-73 —Emily

COLLEGE
West Virginia — Bob
Shepherd College — Emily

EMILY'S OCCUPATION
Campus manager for
Communities in Schools

Emily and Bob Haas at 4-H Camp.

All children should be taught to
"Respect." — Bob
"Set goals, and strive to achieve." — Emily

This makes me smile
"4-H Camp, and Kevin Smith's story about T-Bone." — Bob
"Spending time with my family." — Emily

If you were stranded on a desert island, three things you would take with you
"My wife, toothbrush, and toothpaste." — Bob
"My husband, music, and a book." —Emily

If you could leave one thing behind for the world to learn from life, it would be
"Live each day as though it is your last." — Bob
"Treat each day as a gift." — Emily

Our plans for the future are
"Children, and retire to a log cabin in the woods." — Bob & Emily

My hero/heroes are
"John Spiker, Jeff Orndorff, Diane Hayes, Mom, and Dad." — Bob

My favorite books/authors are
"Books: *A Touch of Charisma*, by Guy H. Stewart." — Bob
"*The Giving Tree,* by Shel Silverstein." — Emily

Favorite food/meal
"Hot rolls, mashed potatoes and gravy, and roast beef—served at Jackson's Mill." — Bob
"Edamame." — Emily

I wish I could sing like
"Master P." — Bob

My friends call me (nickname)
"Hoss." — Bob
"Emmy." — Emily

40th Anniversary
1960-1999
DALLAS COWBOYS · SUPER BOWL CHAMPIONS

MAMS TRIFLE

angel pound cake
³/₄ cup cream sherry, divided
1¹/₂ cups fresh strawberries, halved
trifle custard

1 cup strawberry preserves
1¹/₂ cups whipping cream
¹/₄ cup, plus 2 tablespoons, sifted powdered
    sugar

Slice pound cake, and discard crust. Line bottom of trifle bowl with ¹/₃ cake slices; sprinkle with ¹/₄ cup sherry. Arrange strawberry halves, cut side out, around lower edges of bowl. Spoon 2 cups of custard over cake slices. Place ¹/₂ of remaining cake slices over custard. Spread strawberry preserves over cake. Top with remaining cake slices. Pour remaining ¹/₂ cup sherry over trifle. Spoon remaining custard on top. Cover, and chill 3-4 hours. Beat whipping cream, until foamy; gradually add powdered sugar, beating, until soft peaks form. Spread over trifle; garnish with strawberries and mint leaves.
Serves 14-16.

Alaina, Garrett, Bob, Holli, and Emily at Cannan Valley.

My ideal vacation

"Anywhere with our family." — *Bob & Emily*

Hobbies/Other Interests

"Mountain biking and skiing." — *Bob*

My wife, is special because

"She is my best friend." — *Bob*

My husband, is special because

"He is my best friend. My mother, because she is so supportive. My grandmother, because she is an angel." — *Emily*

I am thankful my parents/grandparents taught me

"Think of others, first." — *Bob*

"Not to allow material items to stand in the way of my happiness." — *Emily*

Michele, Chad, Emily, Bob, Barbara, and
Bailey at 4-H Camp.

KICKERS/QUALITY CONTROL

NFL EXPERIENCE
11th year, Dallas Cowboys

BIRTHDAY
9-8-58 — *Steve*
9-23-66 — *Raffy*

COLLEGE
Dickinson and
St. Thomas — *Steve*
Oxford Institute of Languages
(Milan, Italy) — *Raffy*

RAFFY'S OCCUPATION
International Flight Attendant

KIDS
Micaela (4), Lucas (2)

Steve and Raffy at his surprise 40th birthday party
that Raffy gave him in September, 1998.

If you could put your own message on a billboard for all to see, what would it be?

"Pay attention to your driving, and quit reading billboards!" — *Steve*

"Never say never. . . ." — *Raffy*

All children should be taught to

"Think before they act, because their lives can change in an instant." — *Steve*

"Listen to their hearts, and believe in themselves." — *Raffy*

My favorite books/authors are

"*Trinity,* by Leon Uris; *The Choir Boys,* by Joseph Wambaugh." — *Steve*

This makes me smile

"Watching our kids eat." — *Steve*

"Watching Steve combing and fixing Mikki's hair. I don't ever remember my dad doing that with me. I bet it feels great!" — *Raffy*

If you were stranded on a desert island, three things you would take with you

"A library full of books, a beach chair, and sunscreen." — *Steve*

"Music, books, and . . . a pet!" — *Raffy*

Our plans for the future are

"Raise our children to the best of our ability, and try to keep a close-knit family. Also, one day, try to split our time between homes in Italy and the U.S." — *Steve & Raffy*

Lucas' 2nd birthday party
at preschool (May, 1999).

CRISP-FRIED VEGETABLES

2 pounds assorted fresh vegetables, such as
    asparagus, green beans, cauliflower,
    artichokes, peeled eggplant, mushrooms,
    green onions, sweet red or green peppers,
    and zucchini
1 cup cold milk

1 cup all-purpose flour
1/2 cup grated Parmesan cheese
1/2 teaspoon dried basil, crushed, optional
1/4 teaspoon salt
olive oil

Slice vegetables about 1/4-inch thick, or cut into bite-size pieces. For batter, in mixing bowl, combine cold milk, flour, Parmesan cheese, basil, and salt. Beat, till dry ingredients are well-moistened.

In large skillet, heat 1/4-inch cooking oil. Dip a few vegetable pieces at a time into batter; drain off excess. Fry in hot oil for 3 to 4 minutes, or till golden brown, turning once. Remove with slotted spoon; drain on paper toweling. Keep warm in a 325-degree oven, while frying remaining vegetables. (If batter becomes too thick, stir in a small amount of cold water.) Serve warm.

Makes 4 to 6 servings. *Artichokes and zucchini are our favorite!*

PASTA WITH SHRIMP AND WINE

12 ounces fresh or frozen shelled shrimp
1 cup onion, chopped
2 tablespoons butter
1 tablespoon olive oil
1 cup dry white wine
1 tablespoon instant chicken bouillon granules

2 medium tomatoes, peeled, seeded, and
    chopped (1 cup)
10 ounces hot cooked pasta
1/4 cup butter, melted
1/2 cup grated Parmesan cheese
1/2 cup snipped parsley
4-5 fresh basil leaves

Thaw shrimp, if frozen. In saucepan, cook onion in 2 tablespoons butter and the olive oil, till tender but not brown. Stir in wine, bouillon granules, basil, 1/2 teaspoon salt, and 1/8 teaspoon pepper. Bring to boiling; reduce heat. Boil gently, uncovered, for 12 to 15 minutes, or till about 2/3 of the liquid is evaporated. Halve shrimp lengthwise; add to wine mixture. Cover, and simmer about 5 minutes, or just till shrimp is tender. Stir in chopped tomatoes, and heat through.

Toss pasta with 1/4 cup melted butter. Add shrimp mixture, cheese, and parsley; toss, till pasta is coated. Makes 4 main dish servings.

Pasta with scallops: Prepare pasta with shrimp and wine, as above, except substitute 12 ounces fresh or frozen unbreaded scallops, cut up, for the shrimp.

Mikki and Lucas in December, 1998, during the annual "Cowboys Children's Christmas Party."

First meal my spouse ever prepared for me

"Pasta with artichokes." — *Steve*

"It was in Italy, his first time there . . . some kind of 'sudo' risotto with mushrooms . . . it was actually pretty good for an American bachelor!" — *Raffy*

Favorite food/meal

"Any pasta." — *Steve*

I wish I could sing like

"Luciano Pavarotti." — *Steve*

"Barbra Streisand." — *Raffy*

Hudson & Elsie HOUCK

NFL EXPERIENCE
16th year, Los Angeles Rams
(9), Seattle Seahawks (1),
Dallas Cowboys (6)

BIRTHDAY
1-7-43 — *Hudson*
12-22-47 — *Elsie*

COLLEGE
USC — *Hudson*
Virginia — *Elsie*

ELSIE'S OCCUPATION
National Sales and Service
Manager for Bank One

KIDS
Troy (31), Scott (30),
Holly (27)

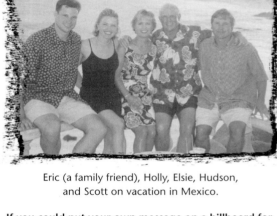

Eric (a family friend), Holly, Elsie, Hudson,
and Scott on vacation in Mexico.

If you could put your own message on a billboard for all to see, what would it be?

"Peace on earth, good will to men." — *Hudson*

"Satisfaction lies in the effort, not in the attainment. Full effort is full victory." — *Elsie*

All children should be taught to

"Know the difference between right and wrong, and treat others with respect." — *Hudson*

"Be accountable for their actions." — *Elsie*

This makes me smile

"Victories on Sunday afternoons." — *Hudson*

"Our family having fun together." — *Elsie*

If you could leave one thing behind for the world to learn from life, it would be

"The quality of a person's life is in direct proportion to their commitment to excellence, regardless of their chosen field of endeavor." — *Hudson*

"The spirit, the will to win, and the will to excel are the things that endure. These qualities are so much more important than the events that occur." — *Elsie*

My hero/heroes are

"My father." — *Hudson*

"My husband." — *Elsie*

My favorite books/authors are

"John Grisham." — *Hudson*

"Sidney Sheldon." — *Elsie*

Fishing in Cabo.

CREAM CHEESE PIE

1 graham cracker crust
1 pint whipping cream
1 package (8-ounce) cream cheese
³/₄ cup powdered sugar
1 teaspoon vanilla

Cream the cheese, powdered sugar, and vanilla, until smooth. Whip cream, until stiff. Fold into cream cheese mixture. Pour into crust.

Add: ¹/₂ can blueberry or cherry pie filling, or sprinkle with macadamia nuts.

LASAGNA

1 package sweet Italian sausage
1 tablespoon basil
1 tablespoon oregano
2 cans Italian diced tomatoes
2 cans tomato paste
1 teaspoon salt
1 teaspoon pepper
3 tablespoons brown sugar
1 container (24-ounce) cottage cheese
1 egg
1 cup Parmesan cheese
¹/₂ cup parsley flakes
2-3 cups Mozzarella cheese

SAUCE: Peel skin from 5 sausage links, and put chunks into Dutch oven. Brown. Add basil, oregano, tomatoes, tomato paste, salt, pepper, and sugar. Cover, and simmer for 1 hour.

CHEESE: Mix cottage cheese, egg, Parmesan cheese, parsley, and Mozzarella cheese together. Grease a 9x12-inch baking pan. Cook noodles, as directed on package.

LAYER: ³/₄ of cottage cheese mixture on bottom of pan; then, noodles, tomato sauce with sausage, and cheese mixture on top.

Bake at 350 degrees for 1 hour.

Holly and Scott in Cabo.

If I were not coaching football, I'd be a
"Teacher." — *Hudson*

I am thankful my parents/ grandparents taught me
"Respect, and how to work." — *Hudson*
"A good work ethic and good people skills." — *Elsie*

Favorite food/meal
"Filet mignon, Caesar salad, and tiramasu." — *Hudson*
"Dover sole, asparagus, salad, berries, and vanilla ice cream." — *Elsie*

I wish I could sing like
"Jimmy Buffet." — *Hudson*
"Shania Twain." — *Elsie*

My friends call me (nickname)
"Hud." — *Hudson*
"Els." — *Elsie*

Our ideal vacation
"Playing golf in Hawaii." — *Hudson & Elsie*

Hobbies/Other Interests
"Golf, travel, and reading." — *Hudson & Elsie*

I collect
"Bunnies and hearts." — *Elsie*

When others describe you, what character qualities do they use?
"Demanding, but fair." — *Hudson*
"Energetic, caring, and motivational." — *Elsie*

JEFFCOAT

NFL EXPERIENCE
2nd year, Dallas Cowboys

BIRTHDAY
4-1-61 — *Jim*
1-21-63 — *Tammy*

COLLEGE
Arizona State — *Jim*
Arizona — *Tammy*

TAMMY'S OCCUPATION
Stay-at-home mom

KIDS
Jaren (11), Jackson (8),
Jacqueline (8), Jasmine
(newborn)

PETS
Moses - 3-year-old Rottweiler

The Jeffcoat's Christmas card picture, 1998—Jim, Jaren, Tammy, Jackson and Jacqueline (on steer).

If you could put your own message on a billboard for all to see, what would it be?
"All things are able through God." — *Jim*
"If you don't plan, then you plan to fail." — *Tammy*

All children should be taught to
"Love God and themselves." — *Jim*
"Respect their elders, and love Christ." — *Tammy*

This makes me smile
"A good joke." — *Jim*
"Funny things my kids do and say." — *Tammy*

If you were stranded on a desert island, three things you would take with you
"Family, chicken, and Bible." — *Jim*
"Bible, family, and good food." — *Tammy*

If you could leave one thing behind for the world to learn from life, it would be
"The way I raise my children." — *Jim*
"Life is short—forgive." — *Tammy*

My plan for the future is
"To be a head coach." — *Jim*

My hero/heroes are
"My wife and children." — *Jim*
"My husband, and Arthur Ashe." — *Tammy*

Baby Jasmine Gail Jeffcoat—just five days old—born 2-15-99.

TAMMY'S CHICKEN ENCHILADAS

1 16-ounce container sour cream, divided
2 cups cooked chicken, chopped
1 16-ounce package Colby and Monterey Jack cheese
1 cup salsa, divided

2 tablespoons cilantro, chopped
1 tablespoon ground cumin
10 flour tortillas
1 cup lettuce, shredded
¹/₂ cup tomatoes, chopped

Mix 1 cup sour cream, chicken, 1 cup cheese, ¹/₄ cup salsa, cilantro, and cumin.

Spoon about ¹/₄ cup of the chicken mixture down center of each tortilla; roll up. Place seam side down in a 13x9-inch baking dish. Top with remaining ³/₄ cup salsa; cover.

Bake at 350 degrees for 30 minutes. Sprinkle with remaining 1 cup cheese. Bake 5 more minutes, until cheese melts. Top with lettuce and tomato. Serve with remaining sour cream.

My favorite books/authors are

"Robert Hughes and John Grisham." — *Jim*

"Frank Peretti, Tim LaHaye, and Josh McDowell." — *Tammy*

First meal my spouse ever prepared for me

"Fried chicken." — *Jim*

"Lamb chops and broccoli on our honeymoon." — *Tammy*

Favorite food/meal

"Baked chicken." — *Jim*

"Unfortunately anything fattening." — *Tammy*

I wish I could sing like

"Kirk Franklin." — *Jim*

"Anyone who 'can' sing, because I can't." — *Tammy*

My friends call me (nickname)

"Abby—because I am so forgetful." — *Tammy*

My ideal vacation

"Anywhere in the Caribbean." — *Jim & Tammy*

Hobbies/Other Interests

"Fishing and reading." — *Jim*

"Working out, Tae Kwon Do, decorating, and shopping." —*Tammy*

I collect

"Kids." — *Jim*

"New series of state quarters." —*Tammy*

Jim's favorite past time.

"Easy going, competitive, and loyal." — *Jim*

"Friendly, honest, and always running late." — *Tammy*

My wife, is special because

"She gives me strength." — *Jim*

My husband, is special because

" He has great character and he loves with his whole heart." — *Tammy*

If I were not playing football, I'd be a

"Entrepreneur." — *Jim*

I am thankful my parents/ grandparents taught me

"Respect." — *Jim*

"To always do the right thing." — *Tammy*

Joe & Camille JURASZEK

NFL EXPERIENCE
3rd year, Dallas Cowboys

BIRTHDAY
6-8-58 — *Joe*
9-20-62 — *Camille*

COLLEGE
New Mexico and
Oklahoma — *Joe*

CAMILLE'S OCCUPATION
CEO of the household

KIDS
Nikki Jo (9), J.D. (7)

PETS
Dog

180

Joe and Camille on vacation in Cabo with Teresa
and Troy Williams and Tammy and Bob LaBlanc.

If you could put your own message on a billboard for all to see, what would it be?
"Just don't worry about it." — *Joe*
"Don't sweat the small stuff." — *Camille*

All children should be taught to
"Listen twice as much as they speak." — *Joe*
"It is better to give than to receive." — *Camille*

This makes me smile
"When the Cowboys win." — *Joe*
"Shopping." — *Camille*

If you were stranded on a desert island, three things you would take with you
"Camille, Nikki, and J.D." — *Joe*
"Joe, Nikki, and J.D." — *Camille*

If you could leave one thing behind for the world to learn from life, it would be
"We are all equal in the end." — *Joe*
"Not to judge." — *Camille*

Our plans for the future are
"Day by day." — *Joe & Camille*

My favorite books/authors are
"J.D.'s favorite book is *Rugrats*." — *Camille*

J.D. and Nikki.

DEATH BY CHOCOLATE

2 packages instant chocolate pudding mix
1/2 cup Kahlua
1 box chocolate fudge brownie mix

2 Heath bars, crumbled
1 large container Cool Whip

Mix chocolate pudding; set aside. Bake brownies; cool. Make holes in the brownies, and pour over the Kahlua. Crumble brownies.

In a serving dish, layer crumbled brownies, pudding, Cool Whip, Heath bars; repeat. Chill, and serve.

First meal my spouse ever prepared for me

"Pasta." — *Joe*

"Pancakes." — *Camille*

Favorite food/meal

"Pasta." — *Joe*

"Lobster." — *Camille*

I wish I could sing like

"Van Morrison." — *Joe*

My ideal vacation

"Relax with sand, water, and/or mountains." — *Joe*

"The beach." — *Camille*

Hobbies/Other Interests

"Checking email." — *Joe*

"Furniture shopping for my friends at Gabberts." — *Camille*

I collect

"Memories." — *Joe*

"Antiques." — *Camille*

When others describe you, what character qualities do they use?

"Passionate and fair." — *Joe*

My wife, is special because

"She gives me unconditional love." — *Joe*

I am thankful my parents/grandparents taught me

"Self-sufficiency." — *Joe*

"Morals and values." — *Camille*

NFL EXPERIENCE
7th year, Dallas Cowboys

BIRTHDAY
2-12-37 — *Larry*
12-14-43 — *Criss*

COLLEGE
Arkansas A&M,
Alabama — *Larry*
Butler, Indiana,
Arkansas State — *Criss*

CRISS'S OCCUPATION
Elementary guidance
counselor

KIDS
Layne (26), Logan (16)

PETS
Sunshine - Pit Bull

Layne and Larry in Little Rock, Arkansas.

If you could put your own message on a billboard for all to see, what would it be?
"We are responsible for others less fortunate." — *Larry*
"Treat others the way you want to be treated." — *Criss*

All children should be taught to
"Be mature. We have to do the things that need to be done, not just what we want to do." — *Larry*
"Support themselves, and be respectful of others." — *Criss*

This makes me smile
"Being able to do things for my wife and children." — *Larry*
"Cooking for my family." — *Criss*

If you were stranded on a desert island, three things you would take with you
"Lots of autobiographies, battery-operated satellite TV, and great food." — *Larry*
"History books, lots of coffee, and my husband!" — *Criss*

If you could leave one thing behind for the world to learn from life, it would be
"In the end, there's no real station or destination—life is a journey." — *Larry*
"Importance of family and love, and never giving up." — *Criss*

Our plans for the future are
"Keep on keeping on with the Cowboys." — *Larry & Criss*

My favorite books/authors are
"William Faulkner, Hemingway, and Willie Morris." — *Larry*
"Mary Higgins Clark and Anne Rivers Siddons." — *Criss*

First meal my spouse ever prepared for me
"Steak dinner." — *Larry*

HOT WATER CORNBREAD

2 cups (or more) Aunt Jemima's white cornmeal   4 cups (or more) boiling water
    (not self-rising)

Add water to cornmeal. Stir quickly, to consistency of mashed potatoes. Add more water or cornmeal as needed. Mold into an oblong shape, about the size of a hamburger patty. Fry, medium to high heat, until golden brown; turn, and repeat on the other side.
Great with southern vegetable meals.

Favorite food/meal
"Purple hull peas, turnip greens,
fresh tomatoes, and hot water cornbread." — *Larry*
"Sushi, Chinese, and Italian." — *Criss*

I wish I could sing like
"Frank Sinatra." — *Larry*
"Linda Ronstadt." — *Criss*

My friends call me (nickname)
"Lace." — *Larry*

Our ideal vacation
"Destin, Florida." — *Larry & Criss*

Hobbies/Other Interests
"Golf, jogging, and reading." — *Larry*
"Gardening, decorating, and junking." — *Criss*

I collect
"Golf balls." — *Larry*
"Family photos." — *Criss*

Logan and Layne at
a cousin's wedding.

When others describe you, what character qualities do they use?
"Opinionated, assertive, and decision-maker." — *Larry*
"Positive attitude, and sense of humor." — *Criss*

My wife, is special because
"Everyone likes her, because she is so sweet." — *Larry*

My mother, is special because
"She has unconditional love, and she always listens!" — *Criss*

I am thankful my parents/grandparents taught me
"To be independent." — *Larry*
"To be motivated, and self-sufficient." — *Criss*

Jim & Rosanne MAURER

NFL EXPERIENCE
9th year, Dallas Cowboys

BIRTHDAY
3-8-65 — *Jim*
2-23-65 — *Rosanne*

COLLEGE
SMU — *Jim*
Texas Tech — *Rosanne*

ROSANNE'S OCCUPATION
Homemaker

KIDS
Nick (10), Ben (7)

PETS
Rookie - Silky Terrier

The Maurers ringing in the New Year.

If you could put your own message on a billboard for all to see, what would it be?
"Be nice to someone you don't know today." — *Jim*

All children should be taught to
"Respect others." — *Jim*
"Rely upon God, and work hard." — *Rosanne*

This makes me smile
"A hole in one . . . someday!" — *Jim*

If you were stranded on a desert island, three things you would take with you
"A sand wedge and 2 golf balls." — *Jim*

If you could leave one thing behind for the world to learn from life, it would be
"A well-worn Bible." — *Rosanne*

Our plans for the future are
"Vacations to the beach, and skiing (snow)." — *Jim & Rosanne*

My favorite books/authors are
"The last good movie I saw—'Saving Private Ryan.'" — *Rosanne*

First meal my spouse ever prepared for me
"Orange Roughy Almondine." — *Jim*
"Jim's special nachos." — *Rosanne*

Favorite food/meal
"BBQ ribs." — *Jim*
"A good, rare steak from Ruth's Chris." — *Rosanne*

Jim and Gran—Jim's grandmother, Frances Rauen.

GRAN'S MEAT PIES

PIE FILLING:
8 pounds ground pork butt (*course* ground, as lean as possible)
4 cups onions, diced
8 cups potatoes, cubed
4-5 teaspoons salt, to taste
3 teaspoons pepper
3 tablespoons parsley

2-3 teaspoons garlic salt

CRUST:
2$\frac{1}{2}$ to 3 pounds flour
2 cups shortening
2-3 teaspoons salt
3-4 cups water

Place all ingredients, except potatoes, in a large pot. Add enough water, to cover. Cook on medium heat, stirring often for $\frac{1}{2}$ hour. Add potatoes, and cook for another $\frac{1}{2}$ hour.

Mix ingredients for crust dough. You will need a top and bottom crust for each pie. (As a short-cut, you can use pre-made pie crusts from the refrigerator section of the grocery store.)

Place bottom crust in pie pan. Fill with meat mixture. Add some of the juice from the meat mixture as well. Place top crust on pie. Pinch top and bottom crusts together with your thumb. Trim excess dough from pie pan. Bake at 350 degrees for 30 to 45 minutes. These pies freeze well.

These ingredients should make 7-8 pies.

MOMMO'S ITALIAN LOVE CAKE

1 box fudge marble cake mix
2 pounds Ricotta cheese
$\frac{3}{4}$ cup sugar
4 eggs
1 teaspoon vanilla

ICING:
1 small box instant chocolate pudding
1 cup milk
8 ounces Cool Whip

Mix cake, as directed on box. Put mixture in a 9x13-inch pan. In a separate bowl, mix Ricotta cheese, sugar, eggs, and vanilla. Spoon over unbaked batter. Bake at 350 degrees for 1 hour. Cool.

Add milk to pudding, and beat; add Cool Whip. Ice cake, and refrigerate overnight.

Jim and the boys.

Bruce & Kathy MAYS

NFL EXPERIENCE
10th year, Dallas Cowboys

BIRTHDAY
8-6-43 — *Bruce*
1-6-48 — *Kathy*

COLLEGE
Ohio Northern - Akron;
and Oklahoma State — *Bruce*
Oklahoma State — *Kathy*

KATHY'S OCCUPATION
Registered Dietitian

KIDS
Kirsten (30), Jennifer (24),
Laura (21), Damien (21)

GRANDKIDS
Molly Jo

PETS
Shakespeare - Toy Poodle

Kathy and Bruce Mays dining out
in New York City on vacation.

If you could put your own message on a billboard for all to see, what would it be?
"Be trustworthy." — *Bruce*
"Believe in yourself." — *Kathy*

All children should be taught to
"Set goals." — *Bruce*
"Never quit." — *Kathy*

This makes me smile
"Seeing others around me happy." — *Bruce*
"A funny joke." — *Kathy*

If you were stranded on a desert island, three things you would take with you
"My Bible, my wife, and my children." — *Bruce*

If you could leave one thing behind for the world learn from life, it would be
"Work ethic." — *Bruce*
"Take one day at a time." — *Kathy*

Our plans for the future are
"To grow old together." — *Bruce & Kathy*

My favorite books/authors are
"*Working with Emotional Intelligence, by Daniel Goleman.*" — *Bruce*

First meal my spouse ever prepared for me
"Chinese stir-fry." — *Bruce*

Favorite food/meal
"Italian sausage." — *Bruce*
"A great seafood meal." — *Kathy*

Jennifer and Laura in New Orleans
to watch A&M play in the Sugar Bowl.

WHITE CHILI

½ cup shallots
3 cloves minced garlic
1 tablespoon olive oil
1 pound ground turkey
14 ounces chicken broth
18 ounces tomatillos, drained, chopped
14 ounces whole tomatoes, undrained, chopped
4 ounces chopped green chili peppers, undrained

½ teaspoon dry whole oregano
½ teaspoon coriander seeds, crushed
2 (15 ounces) cannellini beans
¼ teaspoon ground cumin
3 tablespoons fresh lime juice
¼ teaspoon black pepper
sharp cheese, grated

Brown shallots and garlic in olive oil. Add ground turkey and can of chicken broth. Stir, till turkey is no longer pink. Stir in tomatillos and next 6 ingredients. Bring to a boil; simmer 20 minutes. Stir in lime juice and pepper. Top with cheese.

JELLO SURPRISE CAKE

2 large boxes of strawberry Jello
1½ cups fresh or frozen strawberries, cut in pieces

1 angel food cake
1 large container of Cool Whip

Prepare Jello, but use 1 cup less water for each large box. Mix fruit in Jello. Break up angel food cake, and cover the bottom of a 9x12-inch pan. Pour Jello mixture over cake. Let Jello gel in refrigerator for 2 hours or more. Frost with Cool Whip.

I wish I could sing like

"Pavarotti." — *Bruce*

"Sarah Brightman." — *Kathy*

My friends call me (nickname)

"Sand Shark." — *Bruce*

My ideal vacation

"Playing golf, and sightseeing." — *Bruce*

"Sightseeing, and going to museums." — *Kathy*

Hobbies/Other Interests

"Golf and reading." — *Bruce*

"Gardening." — *Kathy*

I collect

"Southwest artwork." — *Kathy*

When others describe you, what character qualities do they use?

"Trustworthy." — *Bruce*

"Dependable." — *Kathy*

Jennifer, Kathy, Bruce, and Laura taking the New York Subway to Shay Stadium.

Mike & Jan McCORD

NFL EXPERIENCE
11th year, Dallas Cowboys

BIRTHDAY
11-6-64 — *Mike*
2-20-63 — *Jan*

COLLEGE
Texas — *Mike*
West Texas State — *Jan*

JAN'S OCCUPATION
Bookkeeper for IFS Financial
Services, Inc.

KIDS
Megan (1)

PETS
Sheba - Sheltie,
Jasper - Chihuahua

Jan, Megan, and Mike McCord.

If you could put your own message on a billboard for all to see, what would it be?
"Think positive; enjoy everyday, as if it were your last!" — *Mike*

All children should be taught to
"Share things." — *Mike*
"Respect others." — *Jan*

This makes me smile
"Seeing my daughter—Megan, and my wife—Jan, playing around together." — *Mike*
"Hearing Megan laugh and seeing her smiling face." — *Jan*

If you were stranded on a desert island, three things you would take with you
"My wife, Jan; my daughter, Megan; and my dog, Sheba!" — *Mike*
"My family, the comfort of home, and a way to call for help when I was ready to go home." — *Jan*

If you could leave one thing behind for the world to learn from life, it would be
"Pictures from our family photo album." — *Mike*
"Human compassion." — *Jan*

Our plans for the future are
"To buy a house out in the country and decorate it up as a final home for our kids to grow up in!" — *Mike & Jan*

Megan and Mike.

THREE-CHEESE CHICKEN ENCHILADAS

¹/₃ cup vegetable oil	2 cups cooked chicken, shredded
8 corn tortillas (6-inch)	2 cups Monterey Jack cheese, shredded
4 ounces cream cheese	1 cup Cheddar cheese, shredded
³/₄ cup sour cream	¹/₄ cup green onions, chopped
¹/₄ teaspoon salt	1 can (10-ounce) enchilada sauce
¹/₄ teaspoon ground cumin	sour cream
¹/₄ teaspoon pepper	guacamole

In a small skillet, heat vegetable oil, until hot. With tongs, dip tortillas into hot oil. Turn quickly, to soften (about 3 seconds) on each side; set aside.

In a large bowl, stir cream cheese and sour cream together, until smooth. Stir in salt, ground cumin, and pepper. Mix in chicken, 1 cup of Monterey Jack cheese, Cheddar cheese, and green onions.

Pour enchilada sauce into a shallow dish. Dip tortillas in sauce, to lightly coat. Place ¹/₃ cup chicken mixture in center of tortilla; roll. Place tortillas, seam side down, in a lightly-greased 13x9-inch baking dish. Cover with remaining enchilada sauce. Bake at 350 degrees for 25 minutes. Sprinkle remaining Monterey Jack cheese over the top; continue baking for 3 minutes longer.

If desired, garnish with sour cream and guacamole. Makes 4 servings.

SOUR CREAM COFFEE CAKE

2 cups all-purpose flour	2 eggs
1 teaspoon baking powder	1 teaspoon vanilla
¹/₂ teaspoon baking soda	1 container (8-ounce) dairy sour cream
¹/₂ teaspoon salt	3 tablespoons sugar
1 cup butter, or margarine, softened	1¹/₂ teaspoons ground cinnamon
1¹/₄ cups sugar	

Grease and flour a 10-inch fluted tube pan; set aside. In a medium mixing bowl, stir together flour, baking powder, baking soda, and salt; set aside.

In a large mixing bowl, beat together butter and 1¹/₄ cups sugar with a mixer, until combined. Beat in eggs and vanilla, until combined. Add flour mixture and sour cream alternately to butter mixture, beating just until combined after each addition. Spread half of mixture into pan. Stir together 3 tablespoons sugar and cinnamon. Sprinkle over batter in the pan. Spread remaining batter over sugar mixture. Bake at 350 degrees for 45 to 50 minutes, or until a toothpick inserted near the center comes out clean. Cool in pan on wire rack for 15 minutes. Remove from pan; cool. Sprinkle with sifted powdered sugar, or drizzle on icing, if desired. Serve warm. Makes 14 to 16 servings.

My hero/heroes are

"Michael Jordan." — *Mike*

"My grandmothers." — *Jan*

My favorite books/authors are

"John Steinbeck and John Grisham." — *Mike*

Megan McCord.

First meal my spouse ever prepared for me

"Chicken and rice casserole." — *Mike*

"Baked spaghetti." — *Jan*

Favorite food/meal

"Mashed potatoes and Italian food." — *Mike*

"Mexican food." — *Jan*

I wish I could sing like

"George Strait." — *Mike*

"Reba McEntire." — *Jan*

Les & Kathy MILES

NFL EXPERIENCE
2nd year, Dallas Cowboys

BIRTHDAY
11-10-53 — *Les*
9-20-63 — *Kathy*

COLLEGE
Michigan — *Les*
Michigan — *Kathy*

KATHY'S OCCUPATION
Wife and mother

KIDS
Kathryn (5), Les Matthew (3),
Benjamin (newborn)

190

The Miles family (March, 1999).

Our plans for the future are
"Help the Cowboys win another Super Bowl, and do a great job raising our children." — *Les & Kathy*

My hero/heroes are
"My husband, Les." — *Kathy*

Favorite food/meal
"New York strip at Monty's Chow House in Tulsa." — *Les*
"Crab legs with daughter, Kathryn Ann." — *Kathy*

I wish I could sing like
"Celine Dion." — *Kathy*

All children should be taught to
"Believe in God." — *Les*
"Be respectful and work hard." — *Kathy*

This makes me smile
"My children and wife." — *Les*
"Seeing my children smile." — *Kathy*

If you were stranded on a desert island, three things you would take with you
"My Bible, an unlimited supply of Diet Coke, and a pizza delivery phone number." — *Les*
"My wedding ring, picture of my family, and an unlimited supply of orange juice." — *Kathy*

Les Matthew "Manny" and Kathryn Ann "Smacker" sleeping in car while on family vacation.

Chef Grady Spears's
COOK'S BUTTERS

CILANTRO BUTTER
2 cups loosely-packed cilantro leaves
1 cup unsalted butter, softened

kosher salt, to taste

Butter mixed with herbs or chiles is one of my favorite steak toppings. You soften the butter, mix in the seasonings; then, freeze the butter into a cylinder and slice it. It's easy to do, and it adds a nice touch of color and flavor to simple grilled meats. Cook's butters are also great on sourdough biscuits and breads. Here's a couple of flavors to choose from.

Finely chop the cilantro leaves, or place them in the container of a food processor and process. The processor method will give a greener color to the finished butter. Place the cilantro, butter, and salt in a mixer, fitted with a paddle attachment; beat, at medium speed, until the butter is light and fluffy. Remove the butter from the bowl, place on a length of parchment paper or foil, and roll into a 1½-inch-wide cylinder, squeezing gently to remove any air pockets. Freeze the butter, until ready for use. Just before serving time, thaw the butter for 10 minutes. Then, cut it into thin disks. Serve it cold. The butter will keep in the freezer for up to 3 months.

Yield: 8 1-ounce portions

VARIATIONS

ROASTED GARLIC BUTTER: Blend 2 tablespoons garlic purée with the butter, until the butter is light and fluffy. Season it with salt and pepper, to taste. Proceed, as directed above.

CHILE BUTTER: Measure 5 teaspoons of freshly-ground pasilla, ancho, or guajillo powder; blend it with the butter, until light and fluffy. Season the butter with salt and pepper, to taste. Proceed, as directed above.

My friends call me (nickname)

"My kids call me Big Daddy." — *Les*

"My kids call me Smacks." — *Kathy*

My ideal vacation

"Don't know—haven't taken it yet." — *Les*

"Sun, working out at a health spa, and good food with family." — *Kathy*

Benny likes to drive—family vacation, 1999 (the car is in park!).

Hobbies/Other Interests

"Running, watching kids play sports, coach/pitch softball, golf, and movies." — *Les*

"Running, and watching kids play sports." — *Kathy*

When others describe you, what character qualities do they use?

"Friendly, outgoing, loyal, and loves his family." — *Les*

"Honest, loyal, and athletic." — *Kathy*

If I were not coaching football, I'd be a

"A lawyer." — *Les*

I am thankful my parents/ grandparents taught me

"Hang on to life with both hands, and be aggressive." — *Les*

"To never quit, work hard, and be loyal." — *Kathy*

Dwain & Cathy PAINTER

NFL EXPERIENCE
11th year, Pittsburgh Steelers
(4), Indianapolis Colts (2),
San Diego Chargers (3),
Denver Broncos (1),
Dallas Cowboys

BIRTHDAY
2-13-42 — *Dwain*
9-28-43 — *Cathy*

COLLEGE
Rutgers — *Dwain*

CATHY'S OCCUPATION
Retired

KIDS
Gary (36), Michael (33),
Christine (30), Doug (27)

GRANDKIDS
Taylor (6), Derek (5), Shane (1),
Brittany (newborn), Jason
(newborn)

192

Family photo of our son Doug's wedding
to Lisa. They're all married now!

If you could put your own message on a billboard for all to see, what would it be?
"Play to win!" — *Dwain*
"Live every day to its fullest!" — *Cathy*

All children should be taught to
"Be respectful, responsible, and to develop a passion for life." — *Dwain*
"Be sensitive to others." — *Cathy*

This makes me smile
"When the Cowboys win!" — *Dwain*
"Watching our grandchildren." — *Cathy*

If you were stranded on a desert island, three things you would take with you
"Food, TV with remote, and a survival kit!" — *Dwain*
"Family pictures, books, and a survival kit!" — *Cathy*

If you could leave one thing behind for the world to learn from life, it would be
"A video of 'Life is Beautiful.'" — *Dwain & Cathy*

Our plans for the future are
"Work hard, be successful, retire, spend time with family, travel, and, at all times, enjoy life." — *Dwain & Cathy*

The Painter's grandchildren.

PRETZEL SALAD

2 cups crushed pretzels, shake salt off
2 sticks melted margarine
$\frac{1}{2}$ cup sugar
8-ounce package cream cheese

1 cup powdered sugar
12-ounce container Cool Whip
cherry or strawberry pie filling

Mix crushed pretzels, margarine, and sugar; put into a 9x13-inch pan. Bake at 350 degrees for 4 minutes. Cool.

Mix cream cheese and powdered sugar; add Cool Whip. Spread over crust, and top with pie filling.

My hero/heroes are

"There are a lot of people I admire and respect, but I can't say I have any 'heroes.' Of course, Dwain is 'my hero.'" — *Cathy*

My favorite books/authors are

"I'm reading *Midwives,* by Chris Bohjalian." — *Cathy*

First meal my spouse ever prepared for me

"Spaghetti, meatballs, salad, and garlic bread." — *Dwain*

"Scrambled eggs with cheese, toast, and coffee." — *Cathy*

Favorite food/meal

"A good steak." — *Dwain*

"Thanksgiving dinner—turkey and all the trimmings." — *Cathy*

I wish I could sing like

"Madonna." — *Cathy*

My friends call me (nickname)

"Paint." — *Dwain*

"Cathy." — *Cathy*

My ideal vacation

"A great golf course (not crowded) and near the ocean or in the mountains." — *Dwain*

"Breathtaking views, ideal climate, near quaint little towns with good food and relaxing atmosphere." — *Cathy*

Hobbies/Other Interests

"Golf, Nascar, Indy racing, movies, and travel." — *Dwain*

"Jazzercize, movies, and travel." — *Cathy*

When others describe you, what character qualities do they use?

"I would hope they would say honest, hard-working, and someone who you can count on." — *Dwain*

"I hope they would say I was honest, giving, caring, and fun." — *Cathy*

My wife, is special because

"She is very caring, giving, and always there when people need her." — *Dwain*

My husband, is special because

"He always has a positive attitude and enjoys helping people." — *Cathy*

I am thankful my parents/ grandparents taught me

"To have a positive attitude, a good work ethic, and to respect and treat people as I expect to be treated." — *Dwain*

"To be a good person in every respect." — *Cathy*

If I were not playing football, I'd be a

"Playing golf with family and friends." — *Dwain*

Clancy
PENDERGAST
DEFENSIVE ASSISTANT/QUALITY CONTROL

NFL EXPERIENCE
5th year, Houston Oilers (1),
Dallas Cowboys (4)

BIRTHDAY
11-29-67

COLLEGE
Arizona

If you could put your own message on a billboard for all to see, what would it be?
"Be consistent."

All children should be taught to
"Do things the right way."

If you could leave one thing behind for the world to learn from life, it would be
"Enjoy every day, one at a time."

My hero/heroes are
"My father."

Favorite food/meal
"Mexican food."

My ideal vacation
"Bahamas."

Hobbies/Other Interests
"Traveling, and visiting my family in the off-season."

My mother, is special because
"When I visit, she prepares my favorite meals."

If I were not playing football, I'd be a
"Living on a dairy farm."

Clancy Pendergast, and his dad—
at the Kentucky Derby.

I am thankful my parents/ grandparents taught me
"How to work hard."

Chef Grady Spears's
SOURDOUGH STARTER

2 cups flour	2 tablespoons plain yogurt
1 1/2 cups water	1/2 teaspoon malted milk

Combine all of the ingredients in a mixer fitted with the paddle attachment. Blend, on low speed, for 3 minutes. Pour the mixture into a container; cover it loosely with plastic wrap. Let the starter sit at room temperature for several days before using, stirring it every couple of days. Each time you use some starter, you must "feed" the original mixture with a new mixture equal to the amount used. Putting the mixture in the refrigerator will stop the development of the starter. If you will not use it for long periods of time, store it in the refrigerator; take it back out to redevelop before use. The mixture should have a sour smell. The recipe may be doubled for the first time. Then, make smaller batches later to feed the original.

Yield: 3 cups.

▲.Delta Air Lines

is proud to be a supporter of

Happy Hill Farm

and ***salute*** their commitment
to children.

Bill & D'Ann
PRIAKOS

NFL EXPERIENCE
4th year, Dallas Cowboys

BIRTHDAY
1-19-65 — *Bill*
12-3-67 — *D'Ann*

COLLEGE
Arkansas — *Bill*
LSU — *D'Ann*

D'ANN'S OCCUPATION
Housemom

KIDS
William (2)

PETS
Misha - Siberian Husky,
Kitty - Cat

Bill, William, and Dee.

If you could put your own message on a billboard for all to see, what would it be?
"Call 1-877-NFC-BOYS for your own copy of 'Dallas Cowboys Family Cookbook.'" — *Bill*

All children should be taught to
"Respect others; love the Cowboys!" — *Bill*
"Have good manners." — *D'Ann*

This makes me smile
"Seeing my son laugh." — *Bill*
"Seeing Bill and my son, William, play." — *D'Ann*

If you were stranded on a desert island, three things you would take with you
"My wife, son, and my boat!" — *Bill*
"My husband, son, and my mom." — *D'Ann*

If you could leave one thing behind for the world to learn from life, it would be
"If you give more than you receive, your rewards are always greater." — *Bill*
"Don't sweat the small stuff." — *D'Ann*

Our plans for the future are
"Have another child, and live healthy lives." — *Bill & D'Ann*

William at the zoo.

CRABMEAT MORNAY

1 stick butter
1 small bunch green onions, chopped
½ cup parsley, finely-chopped
2 tablespoons flour
¾ pint half-and-half

¾ pound Swiss cheese, grated
salt and pepper, to taste
Tabasco, to taste
1 pound fresh lump crabmeat

In a heavy saucepan, melt the butter, and sauté the onions and parsley. Blend in flour, cream, and cheese, until the cheese melts. Add the seasonings; gently fold in crabmeat. Make sure to continually stir, to keep from scorching.

Serve as an hors d'oeuvre in a chafing dish with Melba rounds.

My hero/heroes are
"Arthur Ashe." — *Bill*
"My mom." — *D'Ann*

My favorite books/authors are
"Anything Tom Clancy writes." — *Bill*
"Barney, Arthur, Dr. Seuss, and anything else William wants to read." — *D'Ann*

First meal my spouse ever prepared for me
"My first memory of Dee's cooking is crawfish etouffé." — *Bill*
"Steak." — *D'Ann*

Favorite food/meal
"Big medium-rare steak." — *Bill*
"Seafood." — *D'Ann*

I wish I could sing like
"James Taylor." — *Bill*
"Shania Twain." — *D'Ann*

My friends call me (nickname)
"College nickname was 'Thunder.'" — *Bill*
"Dee." — *D'Ann*

My ideal vacation
"Scuba diving in Mexico." — *Bill*
"Relaxing on any beach." — *D'Ann*

Hobbies/Other Interests
"Scuba diving, skiing, and fishing." — *Bill*
"Scuba diving, skiing, and tennis." — *D'Ann*

Dee and Bill at Rough Creek Lodge.

I collect
"NFL memorabilia." — *Bill*
"Hummels, and antique cups and saucers." — *D'Ann*

When others describe you, what character qualities do they use?
"I would hope others would say I was honest, considerate of others, and friendly." — *Bill*
"I hope people think I am loving, respectful, and genuine." — *D'Ann*

My wife, is special because
"She has the kindest heart I have ever encountered. " — *Bill*

My husband, is special because
"He is the most loyal and loving person, not only to me, but to his family and friends." — *D'Ann*

If I were not playing football, I'd be a
"T-shirt salesman in Cozymel." — *Bill*

Tommie & Tonyar
ROBINSON

NFL EXPERIENCE
2nd year, Dallas Cowboys

BIRTHDAY
4-4-63 — *Tommie*
3-22-68 — *Tonyar*

COLLEGE
Troy State — *Tommie*

TONYAR'S OCCUPATION
Case Manager/Social Worker

KIDS
Dantrell (13), Towanda (6),
Trey (2)

The Robinson family.

If you could put your own message on a billboard for all to see, what would it be?

"Nothing will happen to me today that I and the Lord can't handle." — *Tommie*

"If God is for me, then no weapon shall be formed against me." — *Tonyar*

All children should be taught to

"Discipline and self-respect."
— *Tommie & Tonyar*

This makes me smile

"Helping other people." — *Tommie*

"When I am spending quality time with my family." — *Tonyar*

If you were stranded on a desert island, three things you would take with you

"God, food, and water." — *Tommie*

"My Bible, my family, and my favorite book." — *Tonyar*

If you could leave one thing behind for the world to learn from life, it would be

"Respect everyone." — *Tommie*

"Color is blind." — *Tonyar*

Our plans for the future are

Dantrell, Trey, and Towanda.

198

Chef Grady Spears's
ONION MARMALADE

2 large red onions (about 1½ pounds)	1½ cups balsamic vinegar
2 large yellow onions (about 1½ pounds)	¼ cup brown sugar
4 bunches scallions, green part only	kosher salt, to taste
3 tablespoons olive oil	freshly-ground pepper, to taste

Peel the onions; trim the root ends. Stand each onion on its root end; slice through the center, top to bottom. Continue thinly slicing each half in this fashion, to produce thin, semicircular, julienne slices.

Slice the green part of the scallions into thin slices. Heat the olive oil in a large skillet, over medium heat. Add all of the onions and scallions; toss, to coat with oil. Sauté, until onions begin to soften. Cover the pan; cook, until they are wilted. Remove the lid, increase the heat, and add the vinegar. Cook, until the vinegar reduces by one-half, stirring occasionally. Add the sugar; stir well. Taste the mixture; it should be sweet and sour. Onions have different amounts of natural sugar at different times of the year, so the amount of sugar may need to be adjusted, to taste. Reduce to low heat; continue cooking the mixture, until the liquid is almost absorbed and the marmalade is thick (about 10 minutes). Remove from heat, and serve. Store any extra in a jar in the refrigerator; it will keep up to a week.

Tommie and Tonyar having some fun.

My hero/heroes are
"My father." — *Tommie*
"My mother." — *Tonyar*

My favorite books/authors are
"Holy Bible." — *Tommie*
"*Woman Thou Art Loose,* by T.D. Jakes." — *Tonyar*

First meal my spouse ever prepared for me
"Dinner at Troy State University." — *Tommie*
"Breakfast." — *Tonyar*

Favorite food/meal
"Collard greens and banana pudding." — *Tommie*
"Collard greens, fried corn, macaroni and cheese, and pork chops." — *Tonyar*

I wish I could sing like
"John P. Kee." — *Tommie*
"Whitney Houston and Anita Baker." — *Tonyar*

My friends call me (nickname)
"Keyman." — *Tommie*

My ideal vacation
"It doesn't matter where—just being with my family." — *Tommie*
"Trip to Paris." — *Tonyar*

Hobbies/Other Interests
"Singing in church choir, golf, running, and working out." — *Tommie*
"Shopping, reading, and going out to eat." — *Tonyar*

When others describe you, what character qualities do they use?
"Caring." — *Tommie*
"Charisma, outgoing, and very sweet." — *Tonyar*

My mother, is special because
"She always found a way out of no way. " — *Tommie*

My husband, is special because
"He is so caring, loving, and understanding. He's always willing to help others." — *Tonyar*

I collect
"Hats." — *Tommie*
"Black figurines." — *Tonyar*

NFL EXPERIENCE
9th year, Los Angeles Rams (1),
Seattle Seahawks (6),
Dallas Cowboys (2)

BIRTHDAY
9-17-52 — *Clarence*
7-4-52 — *Nancy*

COLLEGE
Houston — *Clarence*
Minnesota — *Nancy*

NANCY'S OCCUPATION
Partner—Price Waterhouse
Coopers L.L.P.

Clarence and Nancy Shelmon.

If you could put your own message on a billboard for all to see, what would it be?

"Life is like a classroom.
There are no mistakes, only trial
and error of lessons learned." — *Clarence*

"Luck is preparation meeting
opportunity." — *Nancy*

All children should be taught to
"Cherish life." — *Clarence*
"Respect others." — *Nancy*

This makes me smile
"My wife." — *Clarence*
"My husband." — *Nancy*

If you were stranded on a desert island, three things you would take with you

"My mother's picture, my wife, and one of my favorite books." — *Clarence*

"My husband, a radio, and Ayn Rand's, *The Fountainhead*." — *Nancy*

If you could leave one thing behind for the world to learn from life, it would be
"A book on tolerance." — *Clarence*
"Sharing." — *Nancy*

Our plans for the future are
"Grow old together." — *Clarence & Nancy*

My hero/heroes are
"My mother." — *Clarence*
"My parents." — *Nancy*

My favorite books/authors are
"Cornell West, Richard Wright, Maya Angelou, and James Baldwin." — *Clarence*
"Robert Ludlum, John Grisham, and Ayn Rand." — *Nancy*

First meal my spouse ever prepared for me
"Breakfast." — *Clarence & Nancy*

Favorite food/meal
"Any fish." — *Clarence*
"Cheeseburger." — *Nancy*

CHILI

1 pound browned hamburger
1 can stewed tomatoes
1 small can tomato sauce
2 cans kidney beans

1/3 cup dried onions
1 to 1 1/2 tablespoons chili powder
1 tablespoon dried peppers, optional

Combine all in a pot. Cook, over medium heat, for 45 minutes. Easy!! Serves 4.

BROCCOLI RICE CASSEROLE

1 package frozen broccoli, thawed
1 cup cooked Minute Rice
1 can cream of mushroom soup

1 can mushrooms
8 ounces Cheese Whiz
1/2 cup milk

Combine all ingredients; pour into a 1 1/2 quart dish (spray with non-stick coating, first). Bake at 325 degrees for one hour.
Easy and delicious!

I wish I could sing like
"Luther Vandross." — *Clarence*
"Whitney Houston." — *Nancy*

My ideal vacation
"Mombasa—East Coast of Kenya." — *Clarence*
"On a beach anywhere." — *Nancy*

Hobbies/Other Interests
"Visiting museums, and golf." — *Clarence*
"Reading, and sports." — *Nancy*

I collect
"Antique wrist watches, and old books." — *Clarence*
"Rare books, and antiques." — *Nancy*

When others describe you, what character qualities do they use?
"Caring and compassionate." — *Clarence*
"Organized, out-going, and caring of others." — *Nancy*

My wife, is special because
"She is such a wonderful person." — *Clarence*

My husband, is special because
"He loves me as much as I love him." — *Nancy*

If I were not coaching football, I'd be a
"Teacher." — *Clarence*

I am thankful my parents/ grandparents taught me
"Respect for others." — *Clarence*
"Tolerance." — *Nancy*

Coach Shelmon and Coach Houck.

Mike & Vikki ZIMMER

NFL EXPERIENCE
6th year, Dallas Cowboys

BIRTHDAY
6-5-56 — *Mike*
6-9-59 — *Vikki*

COLLEGE
Illinois State — *Mike*
Weber State and Utah — *Vikki*

VIKKI'S OCCUPATION
Coaching the Zimmer crew

KIDS
Adam (15), Marki (12),
Corri (9)

PETS
Hunter - Yellow Lab; T.D. -
Toy Poodle

Zimmer crew practice locker room!

**If you could put your own message
on a billboard for all to see, what would it be?**
"Be the first to give a smile
and helping hand." — *Vikki*

All children should be taught to
"Respect their elders, and know right from
wrong." — *Mike*
"Talk with respect to everyone, have manners,
and believe in God." — *Vikki*

This makes me smile
"Winning and competing." — *Mike*
"Our Friday night out as a family, and all the
funny little things our kids come up with to
say." — *Vikki*

**If you were stranded on a desert island, three things
you would take with you**
"A fishing pole, my family,
and a satellite dish." — *Mike*
"My family, our scrapbooks,
and a positive outlook on it all!" — *Vikki*

**If you could leave one thing behind for the world to
learn from life, it would be**
"Hard work makes it worthwhile." — *Mike*
"Just be kind to others, and
you will have it all. Have faith." — *Vikki*

Our plans for the future are
"Grow old together, and
get better at golf." — *Mike & Vikki*

Mike with his parents. His dad came
to Dallas for neck surgery in May.

VIKKI'S SESAME CHICKEN STRIPS

Nippy Pineapple Sauce*
1 package Country Pride chicken strips
1 large egg
¹/₂ cup water
¹/₂ cup flour
2 teaspoons cornstarch
2 tablespoons sesame seeds

1 pint cooking oil

NIPPY PINEAPPLE SAUCE:
12-ounce jar pineapple preserves
¹/₄ cup prepared mustard
¹/₂ cup prepared horseradish

CHICKEN BATTER: Mix egg, water, flour, cornstarch, and sesame seeds into batter. In a heavy 10-inch skillet, heat oil, over medium heat, to 375 degrees. Dip strips into the batter; drain off excess batter. Cook strips in a single layer, 4 or 5 at a time. Fry for 3 to 4 minutes. Drain on a paper towel.

SAUCE: Mix together, and heat through.

*Serve with Nippy Pineapple Sauce (above) for dipping, or pour sauce over strips.

ZIMMER KIDS' PUNCH BOWL CAKE

1 package yellow cake mix
2 small boxes vanilla instant pudding
2 cans cherry pie filling

1 large can crushed pineapples
1 large, and 1 medium, container Cool Whip
pecans, chopped

Crumble ¹/₃ of the cake in the bottom of a bowl. Add a layer of pudding, cherries, and pineapple. Next, add Cool Whip and pecans. Repeat again.

A good party cake.

My hero/heroes are
"My Dad." — *Mike*
"My husband, my parents, and his." — *Vikki*

My favorite books/authors are
"This month—*God's Little Instruction Book for Mom.*" — *Vikki*

First meal my spouse ever prepared for me
"Fried chicken and cheesecake." — *Mike*
"Little homemade pizzas on English muffins." — *Vikki*

Zimmer kids—Adam, CHHS baseball; Marki, HMS cheerleader; and Corri, Best Pal—3rd grade class.

Favorite food/meal
"Mexican food." — *Mike*
"Seafood and red wine." — *Vikki*

I wish I could sing like
"N Sync." — *Mike*
"Olivia Newton-John." — *Vikki*

My friends call me (nickname)
"Zim." — *Mike*
"Vik." — *Vikki*

My ideal vacation
"Hawaii—it's as close to heaven as we can be!" — *Mike & Vikki*

Hobbies/Other Interests
"Golf, golf, and more golf; racquetball; family; and players." — *Mike*
"Mom, wife, crafts, cooking, love people, and entertaining." — *Vikki*

If I were not coaching football, I'd be a
"Golfer." — *Mike*

AMERICAN SUBCONTRACTORS ASSOCIATION

NORTH TEXAS CHAPTER

Metro (817) 640-8275

Proud

sponsor

of the

Happy Hill Farm

Academy / Home

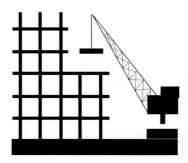

Subcontractors and Suppliers improving the Construction Industry through Legislation, Education & Services.

Recipe Index

* These recipes courtesy of Chef Grady Spears
  from his cookbook, *A Cowboy in the Kitchen,*
  from Ten Speed Press.

Directory of Advertisers

Our Grateful Appreciation to Our Sponsors
from the Students at Happy Hill Farm Academy/Home

Order Extra Copies

The perfect gift for Cowboys' fans, friends, memorabilia collectors, and good cooks

The Dallas Cowboys Family Cookbook

To Order Extra Copies of *The Dallas Cowboys Family Cookbook*

PHONE:	(877) NFC-BOYS
PHONE:	(254) 897-4822
FAX:	(254) 897-7650
MAIL:	HAPPY HILL FARM ACADEMY/HOME
	HC 51, BOX 56 • GRANBURY, TEXAS 76048
INTERNET:	www.weblifepro.com/happyhill

Please enclose $19.95 per book, plus $6.00 postage/handling for the first book.
Add an extra $2 postage/handling for each additional book ordered.
Books will be shipped USPS Priority Mail. Please allow 2-3 weeks for delivery.

QUANTITY _____ TOTAL AMOUNT ENCLOSED $ _____

NAME _____

ADDRESS _____

CITY, STATE, ZIP _____

CREDIT CARD NUMBER _____

❑ MASTERCARD ❑ VISA EXP. DATE _____

SIGNATURE _____